The Gardens of Salem

The Landscape History of a Moravian Town in North Carolina

We hope to see you in the gardens.

Darrell Spencer

Virginia Weiler

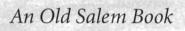
An Old Salem Book

The Gardens of Salem

The Landscape History of a Moravian Town in North Carolina

by Darrell Spencer
Photographs of the gardens by Virginia R. Weiler

Translations and identifications of the plants lists for the
Hortus Medicus and the Upland Garden (pp. 87–89)
© Flora Ann Bynum, 1979.

The publication of this book has been made possible in part
by a generous grant from the Twin City Garden Club, Winston-Salem, North Carolina, on the occasion of its hosting
the Garden Club of America, Zone VII, 1997 meeting.

Printed in Mexico

Spencer, Darrell, 1958–
     The gardens of Salem : the landscape history of a
  Moravian town in North Carolina / by Darrell Spencer ;
  photographs of the gardens by Virginia R. Weiler.
          p.   cm.
     Includes bibliographical references.
     ISBN 1-879704-01-3 (pbk. : alk paper)
     1. Gardens—North Carolina—Salem—History.
  2. Moravians—North Carolina—Salem—History.
  3. Salem (N.C.)—History.   I. Title.
  SB466.U65S247   1997
  635'.09756'67—dc20   96-33853
                                          CIP

*Preceding page: "A View of Salem in North Carolina 1787," by
Ludwig Gottfried von Redeken. This watercolor shows the hilly
terrain and the appearance of the outlots around Salem. Many
of the buildings pictured here can still be recognized today, but
the countryside has been obscured by urban development.*

To Flora Ann Bynum
in recognition of her vision and leadership in
restoring the historic landscape of Old Salem.

'Painted Lady' pole beans in the Triebel garden at Old Salem.

🌿 Contents

Guelder rose (Viburnum opulus) *and lilac* (Syringa vulgaris) *growing along a garden fence.*

❦ *Acknowledgments*

This publication would not be possible without the tireless dedication of Flora Ann Bynum, a long-time Old Salem resident, chairman of Old Salem's landscape restoration committee, and ardent advocate for the museum's horticulture program. A great deal of the information in this book comes directly from her considerable knowledge of Salem's garden history, much of it previously published in her 1979 book, the *Old Salem Garden Guide,* as well as from her numerous articles and the memoranda and research notes she so generously shared with me.

I am also grateful for the assistance of many others. Old Salem's editor of publications, Cornelia Wright, offered guidance and encouragement throughout the production of this book and directed the project in a thoughtful and creative manner. Photographer Virginia Weiler took a genuine personal interest in the publication, and her wonderful images of the landscape truly succeed in capturing the spirit of Old Salem's historical landscape. Old Salem photographer Wesley Stewart lent his time and talent to studio photography and to reproducing historical maps and other archival documents. Other Old Salem staff members, Gene Capps, vice president of interpretation; John Larson, vice president for restoration and preservation; and Bradford Rauschenberg, director of research, reviewed the text for detail and historical accuracy. The staff of the Archives of the Moravian Church of America, Southern Province, especially archivist Daniel Crews and assistant archivist Richard Starbuck, were of great assistance in helping me locate Moravian church records and documents relating to the landscape of Salem, some of which are published here for the first time.

The restoration and maintenance of a historical landscape requires constant year-round attention. For their hard work and dedication during the production of this book I thank the Old Salem horticulture staff, especially David Bare, William Crow, Konrad Gannon, and Scott Sipes.

Darrell Spencer
December 1995

The Gardens of Salem

After traveling through woods for many days, the sight of this little settlement of Moravians is highly curious and interesting. . . . The first view of the town is romantic, just as it breaks upon you through the woods; it is pleasantly seated on a rising ground and is surrounded by beautiful meadows, well-cultivated fields, and shady woods. The antique appearance of the houses built in the German style and the trees among which they are placed have a singular and pleasing effect; the whole resembles a beautiful village and forms a pastoral scene. . . . Every house has its garden. . . .

William Loughton Smith Journal, 1791

❧ Introduction

Quietly nestled near Winston-Salem's urban center, the historical town of Salem strikes a stark contrast to the high-rise cityscape that forms its unlikely backdrop. Red clay–tiled roofs supported by sturdy half-timbered walls and handmade brick bear silent testimony to the unique community of people who laid the foundation for the modern city that grew up less than a mile from the heart of the original town.

While Salem's Moravian founders were busy erecting the distinctive Germanic buildings and fashioning the handmade objects for which they were widely noted, they were also constructing a landscape according to their own cultural and individual requirements of utility and beauty. The Moravians' relationship to the land, as reflected through their town planning, land use, and gardens, reveals a great deal to the modern observer about the values and sensibilities of this quiet people.

This book is about the history of Salem's landscape and how it evolved over time. It is a rich history that takes into account the natural environment the Moravians found when they came to North Carolina, and how their attitudes toward land management and town planning were implemented in the development of the town of Salem. It also acknowledges a few of the many individuals who influenced the process, including Salem's surveyor and first forester and the botanists who lived in Salem and exchanged scientific information about the area's flora with their colleagues around the country. A landscaped central square, tree-lined streets, community and individual family gardens, outlying plantations, and a unique graveyard are living legacies of this particular landscape tradition. Today, this history continues with Salem's historical landscape restoration program.

Vines of bottle gourd (Lagenaria siceraria) *cover a section of stacked-rail fence.*

(Opposite page) Salem from the southwest, by Christian Daniel Welfare, 1824. Open agricultural land and woods surround the town of Salem. Evidence of street trees, fencing, and a forested central square provide clues to the appearance of the early landscape of Salem.

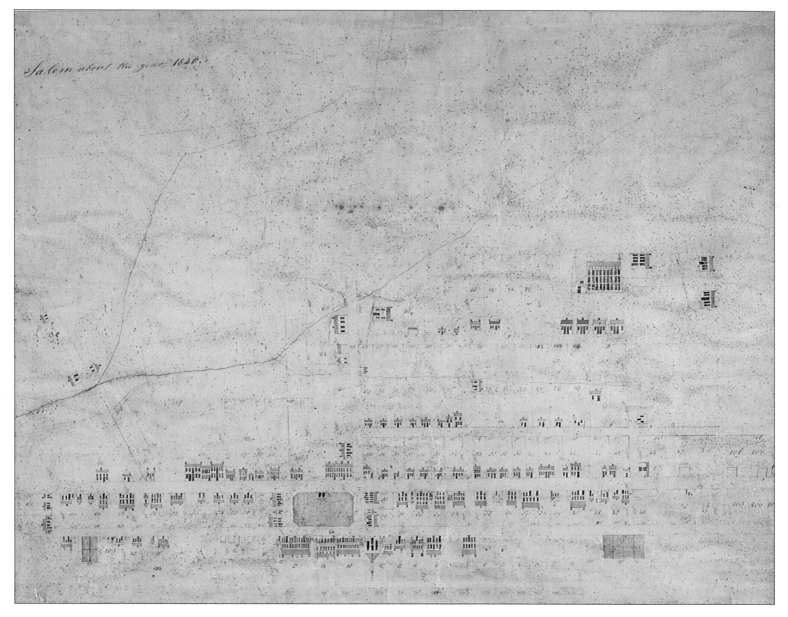

Plan of Salem, around 1840. Salem Square is represented by the large blue area at the bottom center, surrounded by (clockwise from bottom right) Home Church, the Gemein House, the Girls' School, the Single Sisters' House, the Gottlieb Shober House, the Traugott Bagge House, the Community Store, the Single Brothers' House, the Triebel House, the Boys' School, the Housekeeper's House, and the Inspector's House. The Moravian graveyard is in blue at the right, and the strangers' (non-Moravians') graveyard in blue at the left.

Globe amaranth (Gomphrena globosa), *cockscomb* (Celosia crestata), *and pumpkins in the Schroeter garden.*

Old Salem's restored landscape is a living reflection of historical information that survives in the records of the Moravian Church, landscape renderings, personal documents, and a variety of other sources. Today, many of the gardens have been re-created on their original sites. Authentic varieties of vegetables, flowers, and herbs again grow within the garden squares, while old cultivars of fruit trees have been planted in orchards throughout the town and in family gardens. Grapevines and gourds cover sections of split-rail or board fences, demarcating original property lines as laid out by the builders of Salem more than two hundred years ago. Native species of trees have been reestablished in the open spaces surrounding the historic district, and appropriate types of trees, based on historical precedent, have been replanted along Salem's streets and within the square.

With the restoration of the historic landscape well underway, today visitors to this "highly curious and interesting" town can once again stroll along its shaded streets, congregate under the trees in its town square, sample the fruits of its orchards, and enjoy the simple beauty of its gardens.

❧ A Museum Town

The historic restoration of Old Salem covers an area of fourteen city blocks. Almost one hundred original or reconstructed buildings represent the period from 1768 to 1856. During these years Salem functioned as a Moravian congregation town, whereby the church owned and controlled the use of the town's lands, and oversaw many aspects of its inhabitants' social and economic life. In addition to Old Salem, Inc., the institution largely responsible for restoring the town and interpreting its historical significance, the Old Salem district is also home to several other institutions whose histories are deeply rooted in the local Moravian tradition. These include Salem Academy and College, a preparatory school and liberal arts college for young women that grew out of the 1772 Moravian school for girls; Home Moravian Church, which has continued to maintain an active congregation since the town was established; and the administrative headquarters of the Moravian Church in America, Southern Province, which oversees the activities of Moravian congregations from Virginia to Florida. Approximately two-thirds of the restored houses are owned and occupied by individuals who make the historic district their home. Unlike some other historical museums, Old Salem is not a static collection of old buildings and artifacts, but rather a modern and vital community with many connections to the larger urban center with which it shares a common historical heritage.

The authentic appearance of Old Salem's early buildings and its gardens owes much to the philanthropic efforts of the visionary citizens who rallied to the town's defense in the 1950s. Decades of urban neglect following the gradual dissolution of the Moravian community in Salem after 1856, along

Citrus (Citrus reticulata), *old-fashioned geranium* (Pelargonium inquinans), *and lantana* (Lantana sp.) *grow in reproduction flower pots in front of a Salem residence.*

(Opposite page) Looking across an orchard and the Miksch garden at the Single Brothers' House (1769).

The Miksch House (1771) prior to restoration.

The Miksch House restored.

Blackhaw (Viburnum prunifolium) *growing among other native trees within the historic district.*

with the rapid emergence of the industrial center of Winston immediately to the north of the small congregation town, undermined Salem's preeminence in the region and sent the once-bustling town into a slow decline. By 1913, Salem had become enveloped by the city of Winston. In that year the two municipalities merged under one local government, forming the city now known as Winston-Salem. Although many of Salem's original structures still survived, often beneath modernized facades and additions, much of the character that had formerly distinguished Salem as an exceptional cultural entity had all but disappeared.

In 1950, Winston-Salem business leaders, historians, and preservationists, many of them Moravians, joined together to form the nonprofit corporation Old Salem, Inc., with the mission of preserving and restoring the town of Salem. Relying upon the information gleaned from the study of church and town records, personal documents, landscape drawings, and early photographs, historians and technicians carefully restored and reconstructed much of the town's distinctive Germanic architecture. The quality and historical integrity of Salem's restoration were made possible by this vast amount of surviving documentation, along with the large number of original buildings that remained intact at the time restoration was begun. This combination of documentary and physical evidence makes Old Salem one of the most authentic restorations in the United States.

❧ The Restoration of a Landscape

Once the restoration of Salem's original buildings was well underway in the early 1970s, more attention began to be paid to the appearance of its historical landscape. Around this time, historic preservationists across the country began to recognize the limitations of presenting restored architectural elements in a modern landscape environment, and research efforts concentrated on providing clues to Salem's early landscape. In 1972 Old Salem became one of the first historical museums to have a landscape restoration program. Modern buildings, alleyways, and parking lots were gradually removed and replaced with vegetable gardens and orchards. Residential lots that had been subdivided were restored to their early configuration. Historical styles of fencing were employed to redefine original property lines; modern paving materials were replaced with natural stone, packed earth, or handmade brick; and native trees were reintroduced into the landscape according to historical precedent. Utility lines were also buried or discreetly hidden from view.

Any landscape, whether manmade or natural, is by its very nature ephemeral. Its inescapable destiny is to evolve, maturing and changing over time. Land forms are reshaped by the erosive effects of wind and water, while individual plants and plant communities gradually age and die out or are rapidly altered by fire, storm, flood, or drought. More often landscapes are easily altered by people, and their original conditions are soon forgotten as they fall victim to changing patterns of land use, driven by the whims of fashion or the expansionist pressures of a growing population. While the architecture of a town changes gradually over decades or even centuries, and material objects

Corn growing in the Volz field on Main Street, a few blocks south of Salem Square.

(Opposite page) Muscadine grapes (Vitis rotundifolia) *in the Levering garden.*

11

A view of Salem from the northwest, c. 1790, artist unknown. This watercolor shows long narrow lots, enclosed by fences, with gardens located at the rear of the properties.

are often passed down unchanged through the years as valued family treasures, garden or landscape elements can change dramatically within the span of a single lifetime. Town plans or plans for buildings are often documented or can at least be reconstructed through above-ground research or archaeological investigation; landscape features, on the other hand, often disappear without a trace of physical or documentary evidence. Old Salem is fortunate to have ample evidence for reconstructing its historical landscape.

Because Salem functioned as a congregation town until the mid-nineteenth century, many of the mundane as well as critical details of life in the community were well documented by the governing bodies of church elders who oversaw the social, financial, and spiritual affairs of the town and its occupants. Frequently mentioned within the records are landscape con-

Salem's family gardens reflect many features seen in early views of the town, like the one at the left.

The Single Brothers' Workshop (1771, reconstructed) from Main Street.

cerns such as fencing, tree plantings, gardens, and crops. These historical records, carefully preserved by the archives of the Moravian Church in Winston-Salem, Bethlehem, Pennsylvania, and Herrnhut, Germany, have been instrumental in providing the valuable information necessary for restoration of both buildings and landscape.

Other rich sources of historical landscape information describing Salem and its environs include the 1760 notations for the Wachovia Land Register and the 1764 survey notes, both compiled by surveyor Philip Christian Gottlieb Reuter. Floras compiled by ministers Samuel Kramsch in 1789–91 and Louis David von Schweinitz, an internationally recognized botanist, in 1821, recount in detail the types of plants found growing in and around Salem. Their accounts of cultivated and native plants, which include notes on their specific locations and habitats, have been crucial in assembling a historical collection of native and introduced shrubs and trees for Old Salem. Reuter's drawings and plant lists for the gardens at nearby Bethabara, another Moravian community, compiled between 1759 and 1764, reveal the types of cultivated plants being grown locally in gardens at the time and thus form the basis for Old Salem's current garden plant list. Every attempt is made to restrict all plant material in the historical landscape to those types of plants that were in cultivation during the period interpreted by the restoration, generally before 1850, based on surviving local plant lists as well as more general historical references.

Additional resources such as landscape paintings, drawings, maps, and old photographs of Salem contain information regarding the nature of the historical landscape. Old Salem's active archaeology program has also revealed valuable insights into the historical landscape and has often confirmed the exact locations of features such as wells, walkways, and fence lines.

Ever-greater historical accuracy within the landscape continues to be an important concern. As new information pertaining to Salem's landscape is discovered, changes are made to reflect more accurately the town's historic appearance. Also, as additional lots are restored within the town and Old Salem acquires previously unrestored properties, the restoration of the historic landscape poses new questions and challenges.

The goal of the landscape restoration program at Old Salem is to create an environment that reflects the historical significance and atmosphere of Salem as it existed prior to 1850. However, the museum also recognizes the fact that the town is not the same place today as it was when it functioned as a tightly controlled and somewhat isolated religious community. Therefore Old Salem does not try to reproduce the late eighteenth- or early nineteenth-century landscape exactly. That would not only be impractical but undesirable for residents and visitors alike; few would tolerate muddy streets and soggy sidewalks. Instead, the museum staff strives to restore or re-create documented historical landscape features that not only complement the area's historical ambience, but also conform to the town's modern usage. The end result of this approach is a landscape that attempts to capture the essence of Salem's earlier appearance while at the same time providing safe, comfortable visitor access and opportunities for recreation and learning.

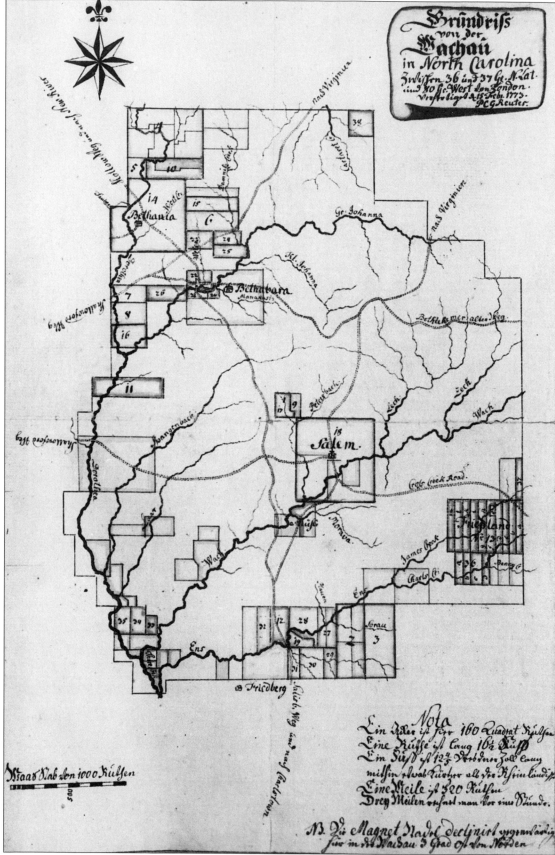

"Outline of Wachovia in North Carolina between 36°–37° N. lat. and 80° west of London prepared on 15 February 1773. P. C. G. Reuter." This map shows the town of Salem at the center of the Wachovia tract, surrounded by the farming communities of Bethabara, Bethania, Friedberg, and Friedland.

🌿 Moravians in a New Land

Pawpaw tree (Asimina triloba) *blooming beside the Fourth House (1768).*

Salem was founded by members of a religious group commonly known among the English-speaking population in the eighteenth century as Moravians, a name still associated with the church today. This Protestant denomination traces its history to the fifteenth century in Bohemia, where it was originally called the *Unitas Fratrum* (Unity of Brethren). It subsequently became known as the Moravian Church, since much of its membership originated in the province of Moravia in what is today the Czech Republic.

Despite years of religious persecution that forced many Brethren into hiding or exile during the seventeenth century, the church remained intact thanks to the persistence of a small core of faithful members. In 1722 the church experienced a spiritual rebirth with the creation of a religious center at Herrnhut, on the Saxon estate of Count Nicholas von Zinzendorf, a nobleman sympathetic to its cause. Zinzendorf eventually adopted the Moravian faith and became a renowned leader within the congregation. It was he who led the Moravian Church in its missionary efforts to establish settlements in North America, where they could spread the word of their faith and generate much-needed income while practicing their religion freely.

One unique aspect of Moravian community life was the assignment of all members of the church into choirs, or spiritual families within the congregation, based on their age, sex, and marital status. Various choirs included married men, married women, young children, unmarried men and older boys, and unmarried women and older girls, the latter two groups being known as the Single Brothers' and Single Sisters' choirs respectively.

Home Moravian Church (1800) from Main Street.

Bethlehem, Pennsylvania, established by Moravians in 1741, became the center of the Moravian culture in America. The church soon flourished in the New World as its numbers grew and its members' reputation as an industrious and law-abiding people spread. By the early 1750s the church was eager to establish additional settlements in other colonies, both to provide economic opportunities for its growing numbers and to minister among the native population. North Carolina was chosen as a possible location for such a settlement.

During the winter of 1752–53 a party of Moravian Brethren traveled from Bethlehem to explore the western Piedmont and part of the northwest mountains of North Carolina. They surveyed large parcels of land that might support a future Moravian settlement. Suitable quantities of stone and timber for construction, good water, open land for crops and grazing, and streams for powering mills were some of the qualities they hoped to find in a single parcel of land. They also sought to locate their settlement near enough to other centers of trade that they could engage in the commerce necessary to support their economy, while remaining isolated enough from the worldly influences of the outside world that they could sustain their spiritual identity. After months of searching and considering numerous tracts, they finally decided to purchase about one hundred thousand acres of mixed hardwood forest and open land in what is today the central third of Forsyth County. The land belonged to Lord Carteret, Earl of Granville, a descendant of a Lord Proprietor of North Carolina, who was eager to have the honest and hardworking Moravians settle on his property in the Carolina backcountry.

The Moravians named their land Wachau or Wachovia, after Count Zinzendorf's ancestral estate in Austria. This name, roughly translated from the German, means "the land through which flows the creek." Bishop Spangenberg, the leader of the survey party that selected the land, reported,

This tract lies particularly well. It has countless springs, and numerous fine creeks; as many mills as may be desired can be built. There is much beautiful meadow land, and water can be led to other places which are not so low. There is good pasturage for cattle, and the canes growing along the creeks will help out for a couple of winters until the meadows are in good shape. There is also much lowland which is suitable for raising corn, etc. There is plenty of upland and gently sloping land which can be used for corn, wheat, etc.

There is also a good deal of barren land, and it would probably be correct to say that the tract is one-half good, one-quarter poor, and one-quarter medium. But all of the land in North Carolina is mixed this way.

Diary of Bishop August Gottlieb Spangenberg, January 8, 1753

The responsibility for surveying and mapping this large tract of land for the Moravians fell to Philip Christian Gottlieb Reuter, a German surveyor who joined the Moravian Church and was sent to America shortly after the Wachovia purchase. Although not a trained botanist, Reuter proved to be an ardent observer of nature. He compiled detailed lists and descriptions of the natural features of the land and the types of plants found growing there. Reuter described the land as

Not hilly but actually mountainous. The mountains are not higher than the ones on which Herrnhuth is built, or the Bethlehem mountain, however all the ridges are connected with each other. Therefore, it is possible to reach any place in the neighborhood, wherever I may stand, without crossing a stream.

Reuter later asserted,

After the land has been cultivated, one could say that it is a rich land. Since however the Brethren have been the first ones to cultivate the soil, and the rest is jungle, one can merely say that the soil is good, growing anything that has been planted. There is enough wood for construction and fuel. There are also stones and lime for the baking of bricks.

"Wachau or Dobbs Parish," survey notes attributed to Reuter, 1764

Ever-vigilant in their responsibility as stewards of a new homeland, the Moravians' skillful land-use planning and natural resource management directed the settling of Wachovia in a deliberate and carefully executed manner. Reuter produced a "great map" of the entire Wachovia tract that noted springs and streams, changes in topography, different geological features and soil types, and predominant forest species and plant communities. The attentive recording and analysis of all available information regarding the nature of the land aided in subsequent decisions that determined the eventual pattern of settlement and use of the Moravians' precious holding.

Dogwood (Cornus florida) *blooming in the tavern field.*

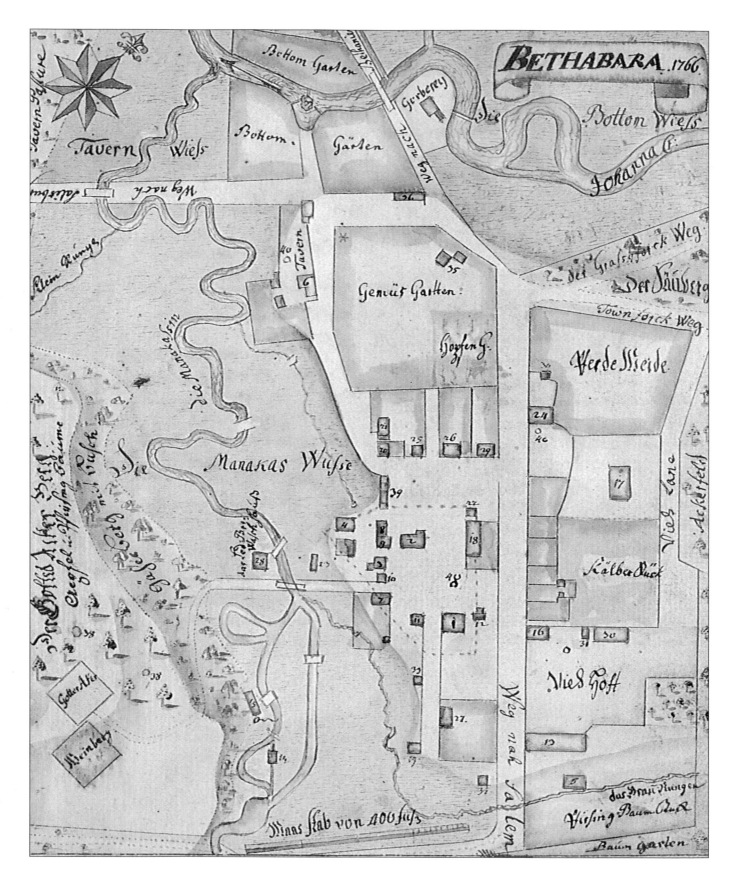

✤ Bethabara: Gardening in Community

In October 1753, fifteen Brethren traveled from Bethlehem Pennsylvania, to North Carolina to begin laying the groundwork for a new community in Wachovia. When they arrived on November 17, they chose to establish their first settlement near a small abandoned log cabin in an area they named Bethabara, a Hebrew word meaning "house of passage." From the beginning, Bethabara was to be a temporary town, a fortification in the woods from which to build what would later be the central town of Salem. Jacob Lung, whose occupation was listed as a gardener, was among the initial group to arrive in Bethabara. His first order of business was to establish fields and gardens for the production of food.

Within just three weeks of their arrival, the men cleared and prepared land on which they sowed wheat, and by the following spring they planted their first turnips, corn, pumpkins, beans, and other garden vegetables. One of the Brethren, writing to another in Bethlehem on April 4, 1754, reported:

We shall plant early corn, about 15 or 20 acres. We have already planted many beans, sowed peas, and other vegetables; pumpkins and melons have been planted. I planted 150 peach trees and grafted 40 apple twigs on wild apples and they are growing nicely.

Jacob Loesch to Peter Baehler

The Bethabara settlement is unique among Moravian communities in Wachovia because of the common system of housekeeping, or *Oeconomie,* that its inhabitants practiced in the early years. Under this organization of labor, the settlers lived communally and worked together for the good of the entire group, sharing the tasks of building, tending livestock, and growing

'Red Drumhead' cabbage

(Opposite page) *Map of Bethabara, 1766, drawn by Christian Reuter. The large vegetable garden (Gemüs Gartten), identified in Reuter's 1759 garden plans as the Upland Garden, is at the center, with the hops garden (Höpfen G.) in its lower right-hand corner. Above the vegetable garden on both sides of the creek lies the Bottom Garden. A summer house is located on an island in the middle of the creek. The Medical Garden, which is not labeled on the map, would have been located within the vegetable garden just above the hops garden.*

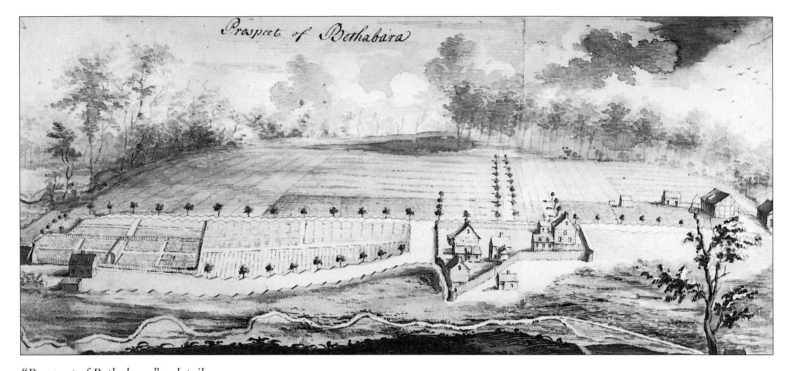

"Prospect of Bethabara," a detail
of a c. 1758–59 map of Bethabara,
illustrates the community gardens of the village. The Upland
Garden, or vegetable garden, is
divided into squares and enclosed
by picket fences at the far left. A
grape arbor runs through its center. Above the vegetable garden is
the medical garden, to the right is
the bean and hops garden, and
above it the hops and potato garden. The entire complex of gardens is enclosed with a snake-rail
fence and edged with trees planted at regular intervals. Grain
fields are neatly laid out beyond
the gardens.

food. They also gardened together in a large complex of community gardens.
According to various documents that survive concerning Bethabara, the gardens
included areas described as the Upland Garden and Bottom Garden, the Medical
Garden, a bean and hops garden, and a hops and potato garden. In addition, separate areas were used for orchards and field crops. Christian Reuter mapped the
general layout of the Bethabara settlement in 1766, including its community gardens. He also made detailed drawings of both the Upland Garden and the Medical Garden, complete with plant lists indicating what types of plants were being
grown by the Moravians at that particular time.

Reuter's 1759 drawing of the Upland Garden in Bethabara (opposite) showed a
large vegetable garden composed of nine rectangular squares, surrounded by border
beds and enclosed on three sides by a live hedge of blood twig or European dogwood
(*Cornus sanguinea*). According to Reuter's notation, it was flanked on the southeast
by the bean and hops garden, on the south by the hops and potato garden, and to the
northeast by the Medical Garden. The plan also showed a grape arbor and a summerhouse within the garden.

The plant list that accompanied the drawing indicated that most of the half-acre
garden was at that time devoted to growing vegetable crops, with only a few ornamental plantings of daffodils, clove pinks, and lilacs around the summerhouse. Small
plots planted with seed brought from Germany suggest that these crops were being
grown to increase the seed supply. Other small beds devoted solely to grafted quince
stems and a quince tree nursery indicate knowledgeable attempts at plant propaga-
tion within this sophisticated frontier garden.

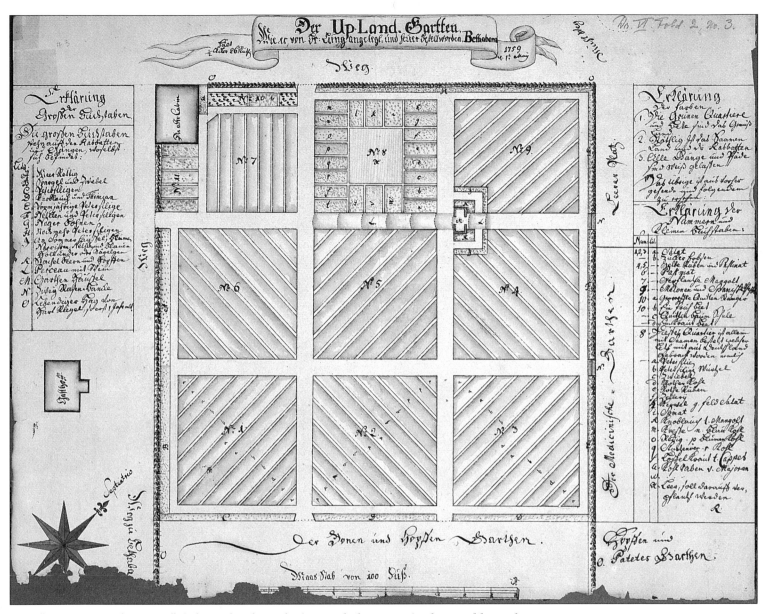

"Der Up·Land Gartten" (The Upland Garden) at Bethabara, a mixed vegetable garden drawn by Christian Gottlieb Reuter in 1759, is made up of nine squares, of which eight are devoted to growing specific crops. Bed 8 at the upper center was used to grow seed brought from Germany, while the small beds around bed 7 were used for nursery activities. The garden is bordered at the top and to the left by roads or lanes; to the bottom by the bean and hops garden; and to the right (from top to bottom) by an area identified as "empty," the Medical Garden, and the hops and potato garden. The summer house and grape arbor (M) and (L) would have offered cool shade as well as support for vining plants. To the left of the garden is Bethabara tavern. The upper left corner of the garden is formed by a cabin that the Moravians discovered on the site when they first came to Bethabara from Pennsylvania. A translation of the plant lists is found in the appendix on page 87.

Fennel (Foeniculum vulgare) *and yarrow* (Achillea filipendulina).

In recent years, much speculation has focused on the Upland Garden's diagonal bed arrangement. While combinations of squares crossed by diagonal lines have been used in gardens since ancient times, the Upland Garden's wide diagonal planting beds are unusual for a utilitarian vegetable garden of the period. Theories about why Jacob Lung chose to lay out the garden in this manner have suggested an improved system of drainage for the planting beds, the advantages of having different sizes of beds for growing various quantities of different crops, aligning the beds on a north-south and east-west axis, and purely aesthetic considerations. At this time such theories remain mere speculation, and no definitive rationale for such a design has been discovered.

Another community garden in Bethabara, the Medical Garden, located directly adjacent to the Upland Garden, was mapped by Reuter in 1761. Labeled *Hortus Medicus* by Reuter, the garden contained a wide selection of medicinal plants of the day. Reminiscent of botanic and physic gardens of medieval Europe, the formal design of the Medical Garden's geometrically arranged raised beds demonstrates a worldly sophistication. The garden was divided into ninety-six beds; Reuter records fifty-six different types of plants being grown. Some of the plants, such as chamomile, elecampane, wormwood, and poppies, continue to be recognized and grown today for their curative properties, while other herbs, including rosemary, basil, and sage, are now more widely recognized for their culinary value. A number of the plants that are still popular in modern gardens solely for their ornamental qualities, such as larkspur, roses, nasturtium, violet, and stock gilliflower, were also grown in the Medical Garden. It was apparently the doctor's responsibility to maintain the Medical Garden, since Reuter noted that it was first planted by Dr. Hans Martin Kalberlahn and later replanted by Dr. August Schubert.

The histories of the Upland Garden and the Medical Garden are not known after 1772, when most of the residents of Bethabara moved to Salem. While no comparable gardens are known to have existed in Salem, the Bethabara gardens reveal the early Moravians' systematic approach to horticulture and garden design, and their willingness and ability to create functional gardens that satisfied their Old World aesthetics.

The existence of the Upland Garden and Medical Garden plans are indeed valuable local resources for garden restoration, but equally as important, they are especially rare among historical garden documents in general. They represent the earliest known American garden plans with accompanying plant lists discovered to date in the United States, a distinction all the more rare in that they represent utilitarian rather than ornamental garden designs, which more often captured the attention of artists and early chroniclers. These garden plans clearly illustrate the transplanting of

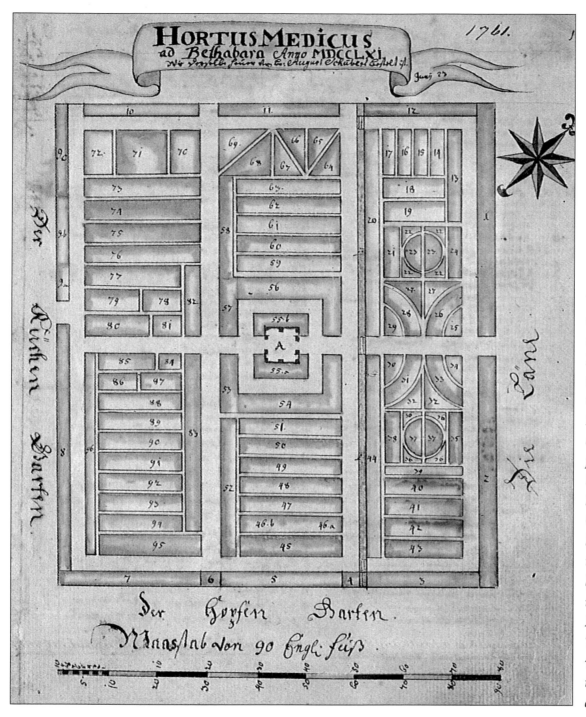

"Hortus Medicus," or Medical Garden, at Bethabara, drawn by Christian Gottlieb Reuter in 1761. The description states that the Medical Garden was planted by Brother August Schubert, the doctor in Bethabara. The plan indicates that it was bordered to the left by the kitchen garden (the Upland Garden), to the right by a lane, and at the bottom by the hops garden. Interestingly, the Medical Garden is referred to as "Hortus Medicus" only on this plan. The plant list, which was written on the reverse side of the plan, is reproduced in the appendix on page 88.

Old World horticultural traditions into American soil by an immigrant population, creating familiar European-style gardens composed largely of Old World plants, within the uncertain circumstances of the New World frontier. Obviously the *Oeconomie* enabled the Moravians to strive for more than mere subsistence, incorporating beauty into the act of fulfilling their community's basic needs.

A Man of the Woods

I stepped on Wachovia ground; I felt very good and thought: This is the Savior's land and I am going to be his surveyor.

Philip Christian Gottlieb Reuter, Memoir, c. 1759–1761

Few personalities from Salem's early history have attracted the attention and admiration of historians as much as Philip Christian Gottlieb Reuter, surveyor, forester, and naturalist. Eulogized by his brethren as "loving and beloved," this man of the woods probably knew and understood more about the forests and fields surrounding Salem than any of his contemporaries.

BORN IN 1717 in the town of Steinbach in Prussia, Reuter was the son of a surgeon who, after losing his wealth, embraced a life of poverty for himself and his family. Christian Gottlieb, as he was called, left home at the age of fifteen to serve an apprenticeship, and later received his commission as a royal surveyor. He adopted the Moravian faith at the age of twenty-seven and began to apply his trade in the service of the church, surveying Moravian-held estates as well as seeking contract work outside of the congregation. In 1756 he answered the church's call to travel to America. He settled first in Bethlehem, Pennsylvania, where he surveyed nearby Moravian holdings and drew the plans for the Moravian town of Lititz.

AFTER TRAVELING south to join the Brethren in Wachovia in 1758, Reuter settled at Bethabara and soon began the daunting task of surveying the Wachovia tract, 154 square miles of previously uncharted Carolina backcountry wilderness. Though he confessed to being fearful of sickness, thun-

Compass rose from Reuter's 1766 map of Bethabara (shown on page 20).

derstorms, and snakes, Reuter adopted a lifestyle he described in a letter to Sigmund von Gersdorff as "Mondays into the brush and Saturdays back home," which lasted four years and culminated with the completion of the Wachovia Great Map in 1762.

MEASURING 7 BY 9 feet, the Great Map described in detail the various land forms, waterways, forest types, and soil conditions for the entire 100,000-acre Wachovia tract. It was used to record all land holdings and improvements well into the nineteenth century. Reuter's 1760 notations for the land register and his survey notes of 1764 include a thorough accounting and description of both wild and cultivated plants found growing on the land, as well as descriptions of all animals within the region.

IN ADDITION to his duties as surveyor, Reuter fulfilled other official roles that took advantage of his knowledge and familiarity with the land and the natural resources it contained. Shortly after arriving in Bethabara, he was appointed Forest and Hunting Inspector of Wachovia, a responsibility that included not only superintending the cutting of timber based on its type, quality, and intended purpose, but also supervising and regulating all hunting on the property and overseeing all digging of clay and gathering of stone.

REUTER MOVED to Salem with his wife, Anna Catherina Antes Kalberlahn, in 1772 and lived there until his death in 1777, continuing to work as surveyor, chief forester, and church official. His vivid descriptions of the forests and fields surrounding Salem continue to inspire the imagination of those who wish to envision the Moravian land prior its settlement. His surviving drawings, including the Great Map and his renderings of the gardens at Bethabara, help us to understand more fully the Moravians' calculated approach to resource management and land development as they methodically set about the task of manifesting their own vision of a utopian community within the wilds of North Carolina.

The parallel ruler and transit used by Reuter to survey the Moravian holdings in Wachovia.

🌿 Salem: "Every House Has Its Garden"

In January 1766, thirteen years after coming to North Carolina, the Moravians began to build what was to be the central town of Salem. Located about six miles from Bethabara, Salem was centrally located in the Wachovia tract and was intended from the outset to be a hub of trade and commerce, a town built "not for farmers, but for those with trades." Salem would also be the seat of authority for the church's administrative body, from which it would oversee the affairs of the congregation and its extensive holdings.

The site selected for Salem was located on a south-sloping ridge covered with thick forest. Its relatively high elevation above the surrounding countryside, its protection from northerly winds, and the availability of a reliable supply of good drinking water from a strong spring located on a hill to the north of the town all made the site particularly favorable. Giant chestnuts, towering hickories, ashes, and stately oaks grew along the well-drained slopes. In the valleys, sycamores, poplars, and black walnuts flourished. Because the town was to be located at the convergence of three streams that flowed into the Wach, or Salem Creek, the proximity of adequate water power would also prove valuable for mills that could serve the local population.

The maps reproduced on pages 4 and 31 illustrate the formal grid pattern upon which Salem's town plan was based. The main street was located along the crest of the ridge, forming the central north-south axis for the town. To the north the road led to Bethabara and Virginia, to the south to Salisbury and on to Charleston. The primary road leading into the town from the west intersected Main Street at the center of town, forming one

Tree peonies (Paeonia suffruticosa) *bloom at the base of a guelder rose.*

(Opposite page) Vegetables and ornamental plants grow together in the Levering and Leinbach gardens, two of the restored family gardens in Old Salem.

29

of the corners for the town square. Around the square were located Salem's major public buildings, including the Gemein Haus (or congregation house), the Single Brothers' House, the Single Sisters' House, and the community store.

Though Salem's town center was never much larger than what is seen today within the historic district, its corporate boundaries initially encompassed an area of about 300 acres. The cluster of streets and buildings now known as Old Salem was located near the center of this parcel. Just north of the town rose a forested ridge, where the headwaters for the streams that provided Salem with a source of power and drinking water originated. To the south, beyond Salem Creek at the foot of the hill, lay forest and farmlands. The lands dropped off abruptly to the east, forming a deep ravine behind the Single Sisters' House. Here Salem's potters mined the clay for their thriving businesses, which supplied popular ceramic wares for the Moravians and their neighbors alike. Further to the east were more fields and forests, including the farm of the Single Sisters. To the west the land sloped gradually to Town Run creek, which converged with Tanner's Run creek at Tar Branch before emptying into Salem Creek. Along the banks of Tanner's Run the Moravians established Salem's first industrial complex, consisting of a tannery, brewery, and slaughterhouse. Beyond Tanner's Run lay the farmland of the Single Brothers, along with other agricultural lands that were leased to individual families.

Because Salem was a planned congregation town in which the church owned and controlled all of the land, there appears to have been a fairly consistent settlement plan throughout the community. Residential lots were all about the same size, approximately 67 by 197 feet; individual householders leased these lots from the church, owning only their houses and any other improvements they made to the land.

(Opposite page) *Map of Salem in 1773, by Christian Reuter. The town plan consisted of a network of primary and secondary streets laid out on a grid system around a central square. Important public buildings were positioned on primary streets adjacent to the square. Private residential lots, all approximately the same size, were located in the town, while agricultural outlots or plantations were established on the periphery.*

Strict building codes regulated the development of all properties, resulting in a common land use pattern among all private households. The narrow lots extended the entire width of the block, all the way to the next street. They were enclosed by a fence for privacy and to keep children in and stray animals out. Since the houses faced directly on the street, immediately behind the house was a yard or service area in which domestic chores like washing, soapmaking, or baking were performed. Wood was usually stored in the yard near the rear entrance to the house; the area was kept neat and clean by frequently raking or sweeping the bare earth. To the rear of the yard were located outbuildings such as a woodshed, granary, barn, chicken house, and privy. Directly beyond the yard, separated by a fence, lay the garden that provided much of the food for the family.

Though Salem was planned as a center of trade and commerce and not as an agricultural community, its planners recognized that every household, at least in the

Salem from the west, c. 1852, artist unknown. Garden squares with fruit trees to the rear of the lots appear in the lower right corner. An arbor of live cedar trees, their tops chained together, can be seen as a green dome just to the right of center.

beginning, would need to be responsible for contributing to its own sustenance. In the early days of settlement, outside food sources were not always reliable, a fact underscored by the drought and resultant food shortages of 1771. The Single Brothers as well as the Single Sisters, who lived in their respective buildings and maintained independent domestic economies, were also expected to raise their own food in large gardens adjacent to their houses.

Unlike Bethabara, no specific plant lists or garden plans for Salem have been discovered; however, numerous maps, landscape drawings, and photographs do suggest some of the town's early gardening traditions. Early landscape views of Salem frequently depicted gardens behind houses. These gardens appear to have been laid out in "squares" or rectangular plots surrounded by walkways of grass, tanbark, or bare earth. A slightly wider central path may have provided access for a cart or wagon. This type of garden arrangement was not unique to the Moravians, but seems to have been fairly common throughout colonial America, having its roots in medieval European garden tradition. Because Salem was built on a ridge and many of the lots were sloped, gardens were often terraced. These terraces, reinforced with stone or sod, generally contained two squares each. Narrow border beds frequently were located outside of the squares, against fences. Small orchards of apple, cherry, peach, plum, or pear trees were often located at the extreme rear of the garden or along property lines. An unsigned watercolor showing a view of Salem from the west, from about 1852, on the opposite page, depicts the rear yards and gardens of two houses in Salem that contain garden squares and what appear to be fruit trees.

Initially the gardens of Salem were largely utilitarian, both in design and in content. Vegetables, herbs for medicine and seasoning, and some ornamental flowers were grown together. One account mentions currants and gooseberries outlining some garden squares or marking the corners of others. One of the squares closest to the house may have been planted in grass and used as a bleaching green, a lawn where white linens were bleached in the sun.

Another European garden tradition the Moravians brought with them was the practice of raising field crops or livestock on outlots or plantations just outside of town. In addition to the gardens located behind their houses, residents of Salem were sometimes granted small parcels of land, from one to seven acres, on the edge of town for raising crops like wheat, potatoes, flax, or maize that would have required too much room for their smaller kitchen gardens. Large animals which in most cases would not have been permitted in town could also be pastured on this land, thus increasing a family's potential to provide for its individual needs. Preliminary plans for the town of Salem in 1765 note,

Until the town has so grown that each resident can support his family with the money earned by his handicraft or profession it will be necessary . . . for each to have an outlot and meadow where he can raise his bread, flax, etc. and winter a cow, so that each family may have milk and butter, and perhaps also keep a couple of pigs, and so have food with little outlay of money.

Fredrick William Marshall letter, July 1765

Garden squares in the Leinbach and Levering gardens in late spring.

This late-nineteenth century photograph of the yard and garden behind the Winkler Bakery and adjacent properties shows the abundance of outbuildings and how all outdoor space within the small lots was efficiently utilized.

Three church-owned farms were set up by the congregation as part of the Salem community to provide a supplemental food source for the town's residents. These farms were intended to provide meat, milk, eggs, grains, and additional vegetables for the busy townspeople, thus eliminating their sole reliance on their own efforts at husbandry on their small personal land holdings. Plagued by poor management on the part of the tenant farmers, records indicate that these farms were only marginally successful at best and never fulfilled the original intention for which they were established.

Knot gardens and manicured evergreen parterres, commonly associated with seventeenth- and eighteenth-century European manor houses, did not exist in this frontier settlement. Nor did herb gardens, a largely twentieth-century colonial-

Phlox (Phlox paniculata), *wall-flower* (Cheiranthus cheiri), *and johnny jump-ups* (Viola tricolor) *bloom alongside lamb's ear* (Stachys byzantina) *in the Schroeter garden.*

revival concept in garden design. As Salem grew more prosperous during the mid- to late nineteenth century, and dependable outside sources for food were established, it became no longer necessary for every household to be totally self-reliant in providing food for its members. Some references to private pleasure gardens appear in the records at this time, and more ornamental plantings began adorning Salem gardens, which had previously been solely utilitarian in nature. Despite an increased emphasis on aesthetics, the family gardens remained largely unchanged in character through the years. They continued to function as a primary source of fresh food for the householders of Salem throughout the nineteenth and into the twentieth centuries.

Vegetables growing in the Leinbach garden.

❧ A Shoemaker's Garden

Rain plenty these days; in the fields & gardens every thing grows wonderfully; we get plenty of all kinds of vegetables this summer out of my garden.

John Henry Leinbach Diary, July 6, 1831

Shoemaker John Henry Leinbach built a house on Main Street in Salem in 1822 and lived there with his family until his death in 1870. Like many early craftsmen of the town, Leinbach also assumed the roles of gardener and farmer, caring not only for his garden at home, but also tending an outlot leased to him by the church. Although food sources were more stable than in the early days of settlement, the expectation of growing one's own food had not changed much from the earlier period. Leinbach not only grew vegetables, fruits, and grains, he also kept livestock and bees, thus meeting a wide range of his family's needs.

Excerpts from Leinbach's personal diary from the years 1830 to 1843 *(right)* give some indication of the scope of activities involved in managing the garden and outlot.

The Leinbach garden is one of the re-created family gardens located along Salt Street in Old Salem. The term "family garden" is actually borrowed from the Moravian Church records, where in 1775 it was used to describe the route of Salem's night watchman. Today, Salem's re-created family gardens reflect what we currently believe to have been the styles and plant materials common in backyard gardens within the town prior to the mid-nineteenth century. The date of each of the gardens corresponds to the restoration date of the house it accompanies. The Leinbach garden reflects the year 1822, the date to which the Leinbach house has been restored.

Sent T. Fetter and C. Pfohl in my garden to commence spading; they spaded one square, on which I sowed Clover seed. . . . Lettuce & cabbage seed today, last snow is gone. . . . This morning I worked in my garden fixing a place, along the fence betwixt Mr. Kreuser & myself, for the summer, where it will keep moist, & where, in case of another summer like the last, we may perhaps raise a few beans, cucumbers etc.

Myself and T. Fetter went to my plantation to dig out green-briar roots. . . . Went to view the bottom along the mill branch, so called, to see whether it would be practicable or profitable to make a meadow there as I contemplate. . . . At work on my new hog sty.

During the day the weather became much milder than it has been for some time now. The peach-trees make a beautiful appearance now, being in full bloom. Got a half bushel sweet potatoes of Mr. Ackerman, which I intend to plant, meaning to raise sweet & Irish potatoes, corn, grass, pumpkins, broom corn & everything else I may need, all on an acre and a half of ground.

One of my bee stands began to swarm, it settled on my apple tree in the yard. . . . I was mending my garden fence along Salt Street. . . . This morning I put my boys to hauling dung out on my garden; and after dinner J. Chitty came to haul it on my plantation. I helped him & it was seven o'clock before we were done. I had ten two-horse loads, large loads. . . . This morning I hoed my broom corn which looks quite promising.

Leinbach Diary,
1830–1843

An early photograph of the yard of the John Henry Leinbach house, showing the stable and a shed with beehives.

Like many lots in Salem, the historical appearance of John Henry Leinbach's original garden had long since been lost and forgotten. The garden's current design reflects what may have been a typical arrangement for a residential lot in Salem in 1822, based upon early maps and landscape drawings of the town. The Leinbach garden today consists of six garden squares arranged along a wide central axis with fruit trees and border beds located along the sides. Because the lot slopes to the rear, sod and stone terraces separate the three pairs of squares. The entire lot is enclosed by a fence, as was common for the period.

The re-created Leinbach garden contains an array of vegetables for both eating fresh and winter storage. Cabbage, lettuce, peas, carrots, onions, and potatoes are a few of the more common cool-weather vegetables grown in the spring. Summer crops of beans, squash, peppers, melons, and sweet potatoes are planted in late spring or early summer for a mid- to late summer harvest, followed by fall plantings of cool-weather crops similar to those grown in the spring. In addition, every effort is made to include specific varieties, today popularly referred to as "heirloom" or "antique" varieties, of plants which were introduced by the 1820s. Absent from the vegetable list are tomatoes, since they were not widely grown in gardens until the mid-nineteenth century; the first reference to their being grown in Salem occurs in 1833. Mixed in with the vegetable plantings is an assortment of herbs generally grown for seasoning food or treating illness, as well as some ornamental flowers common to the period.

Yarrow with 'Red Drumhead' and 'Early Jersey Wakefield' cabbages.

Newly transplanted lettuce seedlings growing in the Leinbach garden beside endive and Swiss chard.

Grapevines growing on a fence between the Miksch and Triebel gardens. The Single Brothers' House (1769) and the Single Brothers' Workshop are in the background.

❧ *"Enough Room to Raise the Necessary Vegetables"*

Grapes, 'Catawba.'

The Single Brothers, the Single Sisters, and the Salem Tavern proprietors had extensive garden plots on which they each grew food for large numbers of people.

The Single Brothers' Garden

The Single Brothers' garden occupied a sizable expanse of land, since it was expected to feed as many as sixty men and boys at one time. The garden was laid out in large squares, located on earthen terraces that extended from the rear of the Single Brothers' Workshop all the way to Town Run creek to the west. Though the Single Brothers moved out of the house in 1826, the garden existed in its original form until Liberty Street (present-day Salt Street) was cut through it in 1890. The upper plots were still tended by women living in the Single Brothers' House when it was used as a Moravian Church home just prior to the restoration of the house in the early 1960s.

In addition to the large garden squares that provided vegetables for their table, the Brothers also maintained a tree nursery and an orchard near Tanner's Run. A spring with a springhouse was located in the lower northwest corner of the garden near Academy Street. Peach trees lined the south boundary of the garden adjacent to the community store property, but had to be transplanted in 1784 because they were an inconvenience to the storekeeper. The Single Brothers also maintained an additional 691 acres of pasture land and fields for livestock and crops to the west, beyond the creek.

Julius A. Lineback gave this description of the Single Brothers' garden in a paper presented to the Wachovia Historical Society in 1899:

A photograph of the Single Brothers' garden taken in the late nineteenth century, looking west across the location of the present Old Salem Road. Here large garden squares have been laid out, stabilized by earthen terraces, and fruit trees grow along the bank of Town Run. The industrial complex in the center included the slaughterhouse, the brewery, and the tannery.

The large Garden below the House extended nearly to the branch. Then there was a strip of meadow, or Pasture Ground—beyond which were the stables—and still farther west and south were the fields, or the Upper Plantation. Near the branch, and not far from the street, was a very good Spring, with a rock springhouse over it. Here were kept the milk and the butter; and from here, the Brethren brought their drinking water, especially in the summer. Since the Spring was quite a good distance from the House, we can well understand why each Brother was required to bring his own water and milk at Breakfast and Supper.

Tradition says that both General Washington and Lord Cornwallis drank water from this spring; this is more than probable. However since both the Generals and the Spring as well, are gone, it is impossible to verify the saying. . . . In the southeast corner of the Garden was a Summerhouse which afforded an excellent place for the Brethren to while away the Summer Sunday afternoons and to enjoy their pipes and cigars.

The Single Sisters' Garden

To the east of the square, extensive gardens were also maintained by the Single Sisters' choir. In 1771 the surveyor Christian Gottlieb Reuter laid out the lot for the Gemein Haus, where Salem College's Main Hall now stands. The Gemein Haus served as the center for all church activity and was the home and office of several church administrators. At the same time Reuter also laid out a garden for the Single Sisters, since they lived together in the Gemein Haus until their own house was completed in 1786. A map that probably dates to 1773–1774 shows that the land that lay between and behind the Gemein Haus and the site of the future Single Sisters' House was divided equally into garden space for occupants of the Gemein Haus and the Single Sisters.

Church records from April 7, 1771, note, "All the Single Sisters from Bethabara went to Salem to plant their gardens with beans, potatoes, corn and the like, returning in the evening." And on May 23, "Sr. Anna Maria Quest, with some other Sisters, came here in order to hoe their Indian Corn, Potatoes, etc., but was hindered several days by the rain which fell."

The Single Sisters moved to Salem from Bethabara in February 1772, taking up residence in the south end of the Gemein Haus. Records indicate that "as soon as they were located they began to dig their garden, so that it might be ready for planting." After the Sisters moved into their own choir house on the southeast corner of the square in 1786, they continued to cultivate part of the land beside the Gemein Haus, as well as land behind their own house, extending down the steep slope to the east. On this side of the town they also kept some meadows for grazing sheep and cattle.

In August 1788 the Single Sisters asked the church elders for permission to use Lot 14, which faced the square between their house and the Gemein Haus, as a bleaching green. This land had previously been set aside for the construction of the future church building, but permission was granted with the understanding that "they promise to return it at once in case it should be needed for a construction lot." In 1797, however,

Cherries, 'Montmorency.'

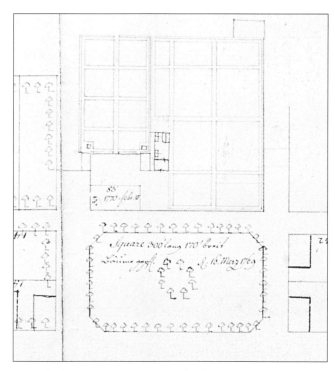

Detail of a c. 1773–1774 map of Salem attributed to Christian Reuter, showing the Single Sisters' garden behind the Gemein House.

The Girls' School from c. 1840, a lithograph by Gustavus Grunewald, with Salem Square in the foreground. The cedar hedge around the square's periphery, the fence, the gate, and the Lombardy poplars are all discernable elements corroborated by additional archival documentation.

when plans for the church were underway, the Sisters objected to giving up their bleaching green, since it had become essential to their laundry business, and it was decided to relocate the church to the northeast corner of the square instead of placing it in the center of the block as originally intended.

The Sisters did not keep their bleaching green on Lot 14 for long, however, for in 1805 a separate boarding school for girls (South Hall) was built there. The Sisters were permitted to keep their garden space behind the school, since they were expected to furnish the food for the students.

The records of July 1839 note, "Since the present management of the Sisters House has extended considerably and the Sisters have enough room to raise the necessary vegetables for their kitchen, the Collegium [a governing body of the church] agreed to have them cultivate the lot behind the Congregation House as an extension of their kitchen garden." Part of the Sisters' garden was given over to the Girls' School in 1859.

The Single Sisters' House (1786 with 1819 addition) today, with Salem Square in the foreground and catalpa trees (Catalpa bignonioides) *in bloom.*

By the 1880s, only older Single Sisters were residing in the Single Sisters' House and the garden had been reduced to a series of squares behind the house, extending eastward toward the meadow. Each Sister is said to have had her own garden square, filled mostly with flowers, which she tended. A common bleaching green remained behind the Single Sisters' House as late as 1915.

The girls' boarding school eventually became Salem Academy and College and its campus spread over the former garden area of the Single Sisters. With the building of Alice Clewell Dormitory in 1921, the last remaining vestige of the once extensive Single Sisters' garden had disappeared. For one-hundred and fifty years, from 1771 until 1921, all of the open land behind what is today Main Hall, South Hall, and the Single Sisters' House had been gardened by the Single Sisters.

Cherokee rose (Rosa laevigata)

The Tavern Garden

Another large garden was maintained by the Salem Tavern, a church-owned and operated business. The tavern was originally assigned a large tract of land that included a vegetable garden, pastureland, fields, and woodland consisting of more than 300 acres. The area included all of the land between West and Walnut streets (except for four house sites on Main Street) and from Main Street west across the creek.

In 1832 a circle of cedar trees was planted in the tavern garden and their tops were joined together to form an arbor. In later years this became a pleasant spot for guests. A young woman visitor to Salem in 1827 described a similar summerhouse or arbor of cedars in the garden of Salem's pottery, which can be seen in the watercolor on page 32.

Afterwards walked into the garden belonging to the establishment where we saw what I conceived to be a curiosity and in itself extremely beautiful. It was a large summer house formed of eight cedar trees planted in a circle, the tops whilst young were chained together in the center forming a cone. The immense branches were all cut, so that there was not a leaf, the outside is beautifully trimmed perfectly even and very thick within, were seats placed around and doors were cut, through the branches, it had been planted 40 years.

Juliana Margaret Conner Diary

Following the Civil War, the tavern was operated as a private hotel. Flower beds with roses grew in the yard to the south of the building, while the garden behind the rear yard still continued to provide fresh vegetables for guests. About 1890, Liberty Street (now Salt Street) was extended through the tavern garden and by the early 1900s houses filled the former yard, garden, and meadow. These houses were removed in the 1960s as part of the program to restore the tavern.

(Opposite) A dogwood tree blooming near the tavern barn.

Spring flowers bloom behind the Schroeter House (1805, reconstructed).

❦ Early Pleasure Gardens

Coreopsis (Coreopsis lanceolata), *larkspur* (Consolida ambigua), *and bachelor button* (Centaurea cyanus).

The primary purpose of Salem's early gardens was to provide food for their owners. This apparently did not prohibit the residents from growing some ornamental flowers, since references to daffodils, amaranthus, cockscomb, clove pinks, and roses appear in Reuter's description of the earliest gardens in Bethabara. Other garden flowers, including hollyhocks, hyacinths, lilacs, and snowball bushes seem to have been common in Salem by the early 1800s, according to surviving journals and letters.

The Girls' School Gardens

A few ornamental, or pleasure, gardens existed in Salem before the Civil War. One of the best documented of those gardens was that of the boarding school for girls. Since the land immediately behind the Girls' School was being gardened by the Single Sisters and residents of the Gemein Haus, the school was forced to look elsewhere for a garden site. The site selected for the garden in 1804 was located some distance from the school along Church Street, where Gramley Dormitory and an adjoining orchard now stand.

A visitor to Salem in 1809 was not very impressed with the Girls' School garden, but he does give a good description of the general layout:

Next, I visited a flower garden belonging to the female department. The flowers were very numerous, but none of them remarkable for their beauty or novelty—the garden was badly laid off, for it possessed neither taste, elegance nor convenience: the soil appeared barren & unproductive, & the flowers by no means flourishing. There was nothing uncommon in the garden. But it is situated on a hill, the

An 1815 watercolor by Christina Kramsch, probably tassel hyacinth (Muscari comosum). She was a student at the Girls' School and the daughter of botanist Samuel Kramsch.

East end of which is high & abrupt; some distance down this, they had dug right down to the earth, & drawing the dirt forward they threw it on rock, etc., thereby forming a horizontal plane of about thirty feet in circumference; & on the back, rose a perpendicular terrace of some height, which was entirely covered over with a grass peculiar to that vicinage. At the bottom of this terrace were arranged circular seats, which, from the height of the hill in the rear were protected from the sun in an early hour in the afternoon.

From the extremity of this place descended in different directions, two rows of steps, & joined again at the bottom of the hill, where was a beautiful spring, from which issued a brisk current, winding in a serpentine course through a handsome meadow, 'til it reached a brook about a quarter of a mile distant. This place was designed for literary repast, & evening amusement—is certainly well adapted for either or both.

William D. Martin Journal

Another more charitable description of the Girls' School garden comes from the reminiscences of Eliza Vierling Kremer, a former student at the school who taught there from 1826 to 1829.

A large garden, some distance from the Academy, was during the Summer Season, a place for recreation after school hours. Each room division having an appointed plot where they could plant and cultivate flowers, many with an innate love for such work would be busy with trowel in hand, striving to have her plot the most beautiful. The second-room girls mostly gained the prize, their Teacher, Miss Steiner, better known in later days as Mrs. Denke, was the Botany teacher and her love & enthusiasm for the sciences inspired the scholars.

There was a large pavilion in the upper part of the garden encircled by climbing roses the lovely multa Flora, this little climber has also passed away, as is succeeded by sisters of loftier names and more brilliant colors—here, such as did not take interest in gardening, would sit in clusters, with book in hand. The hill-side was laid off in terraces and winding walks.

Eliza Vierling Kremer reminiscences

The school gave up the land as a garden in 1858, and part of the property was sold for a private home. The principal of the school then requested and received permission to buy the "pieces of woods" east of Home Moravian Church to use as a pleasure ground for the school. This new pleasure ground was behind the church and included the area now occupied by the Salem College Fine Arts Center, the Salem Academy building, and the existing May Dell, with its small stream and springhouse.

The Girls' School lower pleasure gardens, to the east of the town, in the early twentieth century.

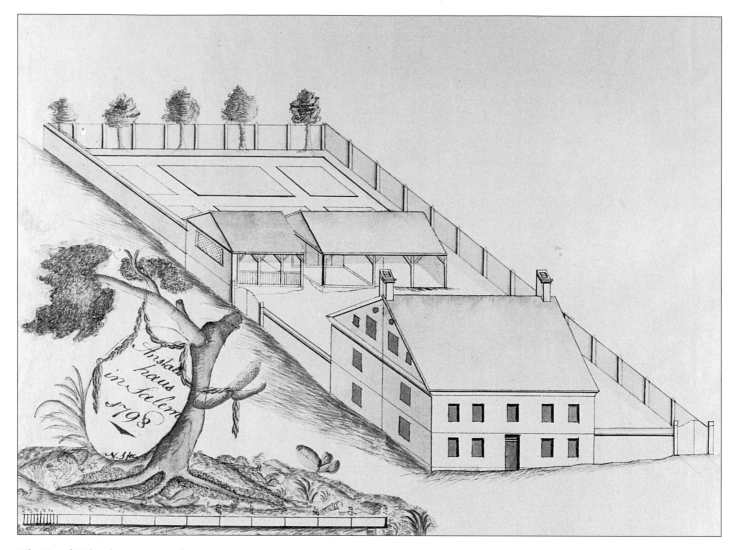

The Boys' School, piazza, and gardens, by Nathaniel Shober, 1798. A series of large garden squares are shown at the rear of the lot behind a cluster of outbuildings.

The Boys' School Garden

Two drawings of gardens at the Boys' School, made approximately fifty years apart, indicate that a garden existed on that site as early as 1798. Aside from these drawings, however, little else is known of these gardens.

The earliest drawing of the Boys' School property, dated 1798, shows a series of large garden squares at the rear of the lot, behind a cluster of outbuildings that included a piazza or open-sided shelter, a woodshed, and a "necessary," or outhouse. The entire property appears to be enclosed by a fence or wall, and five large trees are shown planted at regular intervals along the north boundary, adjacent to the Winkler Bakery property. The artist, Nathaniel Shober, was a fourteen-year-old student at the school when he made the drawing. Whether he was recording the property as it actually existed at the time or whether he was engaging in an artistic or technical exercise is uncertain, since no additional evidence discovered thus far supports the existence

of the garden squares at that time. Shober's representation of the school building itself, however, is accurate and suggests that the garden and outbuildings may also be true renderings.

Another drawing of a garden at the Boys' School was made in 1850 by Maximilian Eugene Grunert, a teacher at the school. Grunert's pencil sketch of a garden to the east of the building bears some resemblance to the garden described a year earlier by Harry Jacob Van Vleck, another teacher at the Boys' School, in a letter to Robert Parmenio Lineback of Bethlehem, Pennsylvania:

James & Friebele have commenced a neat little flower-garden on the East side of the schoolhouse. Br. Pfohl has erected a good fence for them, & they have laid out an octagonal bed. I assist them all I can. The garden occupies that raised-ground below the first and third room windows where the grape vine is.

(Opposite, top) *Summer annuals typical of the mid-nineteenth century, including Joseph's coat* (Amaranthus tricolor), *flowering tobacco* (Nicotiana alata), *hyacinth bean* (Dolichos lablab), *purple-flowered petunia* (Petunia violacea), *cockscomb, and lantana, in a flower bed beside the John Siewers house (1844).*

(Opposite, bottom) *Bee larkspur* (Delphinium elatum), *heliotrope* (Heliotropium arborescens), *lavender* (Lavandula augustifolia), *Flanders poppy* (Papaver rhoeas), *and pot marigold* (Calendula officinalis) *bloom together in the foreground of the Cape Fear Bank garden. Hollyhocks* (Alcea rosea) *and garden phlox grow along the fence at the rear. The First House (1776, reconstructed) stands in the background.*

Private Gardens

The first mention of a purely ornamental private garden in Salem can be found in the Moravian records in 1848 when Lucinda Bagge, whose home was on Church Street north of Home Moravian Church, asked permission to lay out a separate flower garden. Her request was granted with the understanding that she not include a spring and the path leading to the spring as part of the garden.

Two years later, Augustus Staub asked that he be granted permission to rent land for the creation of a tree nursery and a flower garden. Again permission was granted, since the church felt that such a garden "would be a great pleasure to our visitors as well as the citizens of the community."

By the mid-nineteenth century, outside sources for food had become well established and many private gardens most likely contained an increased number of ornamental plants, as opposed to being solely devoted to the production of vegetables. A traveler to Salem in June 1845 speaks glowingly of the horticultural sophistication of the town and its abundance of flowers:

Its style and manners (are) very city-like and no place of the same size contains as many plants and flowers. In every window, yard, and garden you behold them and some of very beautiful and rare order. If a great fancy for flowers argues a corresponding taste for all that's beautiful and lovely, then the people of Salem are unsurpassed.

The Carolina Watchman, Salisbury, North Carolina, June 1845

Although few references exist to house plants or potted plants in Salem, flower pots were being manufactured by Salem potters from the early days until the pottery closed at the beginning of the twentieth century. Archaeological evidence indicates that flower pots had become a popular earthenware item at the Salem pottery by the early nineteenth century.

John Henry Leinbach writes of tender potted house plants:

"February 21, 1832: This morning the ground was hard as bone. During the warm days last week, my wife put all of her flower potts in the porch, where they were left last night & were mostly black & stiff this morning.

February 23, 1835: Melancholy to relate that my Orange & lemon tree are killed by frost."

Except for the increased emphasis on flowers and other ornamental plantings, the gardens in Salem seem to have remained relatively unchanged, both in pattern and location, until the turn of the twentieth century. At that time, the long narrow lots that had been created when the town was originally laid out in the 1760s were subdivided and houses were built on many of the former garden spaces.

Amanita caesarea Salem

Boletus calopus Salem

Boletus floccopus Salem

🌿 Moravian Botanists in Salem

I botanized hereabouts, as much as time would permit it, and found a great variety of plants between here and my former place; though much more difficulties concerning the heat, and especially the insects called Tiks.

Samuel Kramsch to Humphrey Marshall, July 25, 1789

Since first setting foot upon the shores of the Americas, European settlers and explorers were fascinated by the diverse and often unfamiliar flora of the New World. Since botany, the scientific study of plants, only became recognized as a separate science or discipline in the nineteenth century, the study and classification of plants was primarily undertaken as an avocation by men of other professions from the sixteenth to the eighteenth centuries. Physicians were largely concerned with the healing properties of plants, since most medicines of the day were botanical in origin. Clergymen who, like physicians, were better educated than much of the population, also took a particular interest in the natural sciences. The plant world, in their eyes, reflected God's handiwork on earth; its study and classification was closely allied with the study of philosophy and religion. Moravian ministers, educated in Europe, were frequent contributors to the early development of botanical knowledge in this country.

Samuel Kramsch was Salem's first botanist. Arriving in Salem in 1788, Kramsch had been a teacher at Nazareth Hall School in Nazareth, Pennsylvania, where he taught natural science to Louis David von Schweinitz and Christian Friedrick Denke, two other Moravian ministers who later moved to Salem and made their own contributions to the study of botany

Carolina allspice (Calycanthus floridus). *Moravian botanist Samuel Kramsch described this plant as having the fragrance of strawberries and growing in "bottoms," or low-lying areas, "especially near the mill."*

(Opposite page) Illustration of mushroom species, drawn by Moravian botanist Lewis David von Schweinitz while he was in Salem from 1812 to 1821.

Drawing of leaves and flowers of the tulip tree (Liriodendron tulipifera) *by von Schweinitz.*

in America. While in Salem, Kramsch served as inspector or principal of the Boys' School and as the first inspector of the Girls' School. Kramsch compiled three floras listing the plants found growing in and around Salem, two dated 1789 and the other dated 1789–91. All are housed in the Archives of the Moravian Church in Winston-Salem. While in Salem, Kramsch corresponded with some of the well-known botanists of the period, including Humphrey Marshall in Pennsylvania.

Another Moravian botanist, Christian Denke, came to Wachovia in 1820 to serve as minister for one of the outlying congregations. Denke collected plants in and around the vicinity of Salem and corresponded and exchanged plant specimens with other botanists until his death in 1838. Some of his original pressed plant specimens are preserved in the herbarium of Salem College.

Louis David von Schweinitz is the best known of the Moravian botanists. Through his extensive identification and classification of fungi, he is considered by many to be the father of American mycology. His *Synopsis fungorium in America Boreali media de gentium* (*A Summary of Fungi Growing in Northern Mid-America*), published by the American Philosophical Society in Philadelphia in 1834, listed 3,098 species of fungi, of which 1,203 were first described by von Schweinitz himself. Von Schweinitz lived in Salem from 1812 to 1821 and served as administrator of church properties in Wachovia. During that time he compiled "Flora Salemitana," an extensive listing of all plants found growing within a thirty-mile radius of Salem. The Schweinitz's sunflower, *Helianthus schweinitzii*, a perennial sunflower currently listed as an endangered species, was named in his honor by botanists Asa Gray and John Torrey in 1842. Four volumes of von Schweinitz's drawings are in the library of the Academy of Natural Sciences of Philadelphia; the fifth of those volumes and his 1805 publication of the fungi of Lusitania are in the Botany Library at the University of North Carolina at Chapel Hill.

Two other Moravian botanists, Gustav Heinrich Dahlman, who was in Salem from 1799 to 1806, and Jacob van Vleck, also studied the native flora of the region and corresponded with other botanists of the period while fulfilling their appointed roles of teacher and minister. These men, along with Kramsch, Denke, and von Schweinitz, helped make Salem a center for botanical exploration and study in the early 1800s and contributed to the advancement of the modern science of botany. Their surviving floras and correspondence have been useful in the selection of plant material used in the restoration of Salem's historical landscape.

Watercolor by Christina Kramsch, daughter of Salem botanist Samuel Kramsch, made between 1805–1815 while she was a student at the Girls' School. Labeled Serratula arvensis, *it probably represents one of the many species of common thistle now classified within the genus* Cirsium.

Salem Square, looking toward the southwest. Today the square has been planted in an historically authentic manner to reflect a variety of landscape features common to the site between 1769 and 1858. The placement of walkways and the circle of cedar trees are two such features.

❦ Salem Square

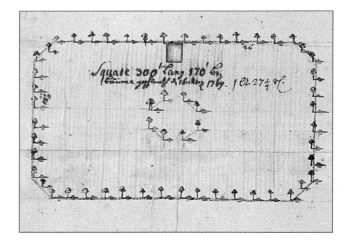

Detail of c. 1773–74 map of Salem showing the tree plantings of Salem Square.

> I am now sitting at one of the windows of my room, trying to write . . . my eyes on the square, looking at the beautiful Cedars and Sycamores, waving and bending their boughs.
>
> *Sept. 16, 1830. Eliza Fannin, a student at the Girls' School*

From the beginning, the founders of Salem envisioned the square as a landscaped public space, an oasis of natural beauty in the center of the town. They planned it with careful attention to both aesthetic and practical considerations. The square's importance as a focal point for the community is reflected in frequent references in the Moravian records to the condition of its trees, the location of pathways and gates, the design of its fences, and its maintenance and upkeep.

Salem Square was originally to be located one block north of its current site. In order to provide a more adequate flow of water to the square, from which it could be distributed to other parts of the town, the square was relocated to its current site in 1769. Since that time it has fulfilled several important functions. It served as a distribution site for the community water supply until the mid-nineteenth century, was the site of a corpse house from 1775 to 1805 and a market-firehouse from 1804 to 1858, and was used as a storage area for building materials for projects around the square. Matthew Miksch, who lived on Main Street, was granted permission to establish a garden on the square in 1772 with the understanding that he care for the existing trees. Miksch gave up his garden in March 1775, and the square was plowed and planted in grass for grazing livestock.

The square was a popular meeting place as well—sometimes too popular, in the eyes of the Moravian elders. From 1804 to 1806, on several occasions Single Sisters flouted community rules by meeting Single Brothers in the square at night. Their behavior caused the pattern of gates into the square to be changed to hinder such clandestine behavior. By the late nineteenth century, the square took on the character of a municipal park.

In May 1989, a tornado uprooted most of the large trees remaining in the square. While tragic, the destruction provided an opportunity to replant it in a historically authentic manner. Today the square reflects a variety of landscape features common to the property between 1769 and 1858. The placement of trees replicates what we know of the early plan, with perimeter plantings of sycamores, lindens, tulip poplars, and catalpas. A circle of trees was referred to as early as 1769, but the species planted there before the early nineteenth century remains open to speculation. The cedar circle that grows there now is similar to the one that appears in the 1837–1847 view of the square by Elias Vogler, pictured on page 63. The market-firehouse and the cistern pump have been reconstructed on their former sites. The paths crossing the square, believed to have been created shortly after the beginning of the nineteenth century, are today paved in brick rather than bark for safety and ease of maintenance. Fence and gate configurations have varied considerably; over the years, the square was enclosed with various post-and-board or picket fences, and occasionally with hedges, and entered through turnstiles, gates, or over steps. The current post-and-board style corresponds to early descriptions and also reflects the fencing seen in the Vogler view.

View of Salem Square, watercolor by Elias Vogler, c. 1837–1847. A circle of cedar trees at the center of the square is clearly evident.

Large trees, including southern magnolia (Magnolia grandiflora), *growing around the houses on Main Street, south of the square.*

❧ Trees in Salem

If there was one resource which the original Moravian settlers truly possessed in abundance, it was the native forest. Given what must have been a daunting task of clearing virgin hardwood trees for the establishment of a frontier town, the fact that the church appointed a forester to superintend the cutting of timber remains a significant event in an era far removed from the modern concern with natural resource conservation and management. Christian Gottlieb Reuter, the Moravian surveyor of the Wachovia tract, also served as Salem's first forester, an official position that continued until the mid-nineteenth century. By "guarding against the indiscriminant cutting of timber and the waste that results thereof," the forester was largely responsible for the preservation and management of the woodlands surrounding the town.

Trees within and around the town of Salem were considered a precious resource by the Moravians, not only for their economic value but for their aesthetic importance as well. As early as 1769, two years before moving to Salem from Bethabara, "Street trees were planted on both sides of the main street of Salem by the Gemein Haus Square." Church records as well as personal accounts contain numerous references to trees and the planting of trees in Salem for the beautification of the town.

March, 1767: This spring several apple and peach trees are to be planted in Salem around the Square, along the street and the two lanes.

March, 1787: Incidentally, it was mentioned that various Brethren should perhaps get together to plant trees on either side of the road from the tavern to the bridge for the pleasure and enjoyment of the entire Community.

Pawpaw fruit.

Red maples (Acer rubrum) *line Main Street in front of the Fourth House.*

A cherry tree blooming in an orchard beside the Miksch garden.

March, 1808: the Single Brethren are intending to contribute to the general beauty of the street by having a line of Lombardy poplar trees planted along the lot of the Brothers House.

June, 1815: The alley of catalpa trees along the garden of the Boarding School and farther south [present-day Church Street] has died out partly. Therefore, we are going to have young trees planted in place of the dead ones.

January, 1833: According to the present situation, nobody should be permitted to build on lots adjacent to Br. Th. Schultz's house toward the graveyard, without being willing to build the house eight or ten feet behind the usual line, in order not to damage all the beautiful cedars.

November, 1840: It was remarked that the Elders Conference believes that we have to see to it that the shade-giving trees in the neighborhood of the Community have to be preserved for walks.

It is unlikely that any original trees or any trees dating from before the Civil War exist in Salem today.

Fruit trees, orchards, and fruit gardens are mentioned frequently in the records as having been common in Salem. References to fruit trees within the town are limited to pears (1790), peaches (1784), and apples (1831), although Reuter notes apples, apricots, sweet and sour cherries, white mulberry, peaches, pears, and quince as growing in Bethabara by 1764.

Trees Native to the Wachovia Tract

Based on Christian Gottlieb Reuter's booklet for the Land Register about Wachovia, 1760; Reuter's 1764 account of the flora and fauna of Wachovia; Samuel Kramsch's floras of Salem from 1789–1791; and Lewis David von Schweinitz's 1821 "Flora Salemitana." This list was compiled by Flora Ann Bynum of Winston-Salem, North Carolina, and reviewed for botanical accuracy by Dr. R. L. Wyatt, professor of botany emeritus, Wake Forest University.

Acer floridanum, southern sugar maple
Acer negundo, boxelder
Acer rubrum, red maple
Aesculus octandra, yellow buckeye
Amelanchier canadensis, serviceberry
Asimina triloba, pawpaw
Betula nigra, river birch
Carpinus caroliniana, ironwood
Carya cordiformis, bitternut hickory
Carya glabra, pignut hickory
Carya ovata, shagbark hickory
Carya tomentosa, mockernut hickory
Carylus americana, hazelnut
Castanea dentata, American chestnut
Castanea pumila, chinquapin
Celtis occidentalis, hackberry
Celtis laevigata, hackberry
Cerecis canadensis, redbud
Chionanthus virginicus, fringetree
Cornus florida, dogwood
Crataegus sps., hawthorn
Diospyros virginiana, persimmon
Fagus grandifolia, American beech
Fraxinus americana, white or American ash
Fraxinus pennsylvanica lanceolata, green or red ash
Gleditsia tricanthos, honey locust
Halesia carolina, Carolina silverbell
Hamamelis virginiana, witchhazel
Ilex opaca, American holly

Juglans cinerea, white walnut or butternut
Juglans nigra, black walnut
Juniperus virginiana, American cedar
Liquidambar styraciflua, sweetgum
Liriodendron tulipifera, tuliptree or yellow poplar
Magnolia tripetala, umbrella magnolia
Magnolia virginia, sweetbay magnolia
Malus angustifolia, crabapple
Malus coronaria, crabapple
Morus rubra, red mulberry
Nyssa sylvatica, black or sour gum
Oxydendrum arboreum, sourwood
Pinus echinata, shortleaf pine
Pinus strobus, white pine
Pinus virginiana, Virginia or scrub pine
Platanus occidentalis, sycamore
Prunus americana, river plum
Prunus angustifolia, Chickasaw plum
Prunus serotina, black cherry
Quercus alba, white oak
Quercus bicolor, swamp white oak
Quercus coccinea, scarlet oak
Quercus falcata, Spanish oak or southern red oak
Quercus marilandica, blackjack oak
Quercus palustris, pin oak
Quercus phellos, willow oak
Quercus prinus, chestnut oak
Quercus rubra, red oak
Quercus stellata, post oak
Quercus velutina, black oak
Robinia pseudoacacia, black locust
Salix nigra, black willow
Sassafras albidum, sassafras
Tilia americana, T. heterophylla, linden or basswood
Ulmus alata, winged elm
Ulmus americana, American elm
Viburnum prunifolium, blackhaw viburnum

Identical recumbent stones mark the burial locations in God's Acre, the Moravian graveyard in Salem.

❧ God's Acre

Tombstone marking the grave of Anna Munstern, one of the first Single Sisters to move to Salem from Bethabara in 1772. Sister Munstern was also the first in her choir to die in Salem and be buried in God's Acre.

Known as God's Acre since its inception in 1770, the Moravian graveyard is located at the top of Church Street and is entered through one of five brick-and-wood arches bearing biblical inscriptions. According to Moravian tradition, God's Acre is more than a burial ground devoted to the glory of God, but, as church liturgy once stated, a "field of harvest" where dead are "sown" to await resurrection "from the furrow of the grave."

Today, local Moravians continue to bury their departed church members within the cemetery. Rather than having family plots, it is laid out in large squares, each devoted to a choir: single men and boys, married men and widowers, single women and girls, married women and widows, and children. The graves are marked with white recumbent tombstones, identical in appearance and devoid of embellishment, which reflect the Moravians' ideal of equality in life and their belief in the democracy of death.

The narrow street that runs along God's Acre has been known as Cedar Avenue since it was first planted with eastern red cedars *(Juniperus virginiana)* in the early 1800s. These cedar trees replaced an earlier avenue of fruit trees planted by gardener Jacob Lung in 1770. The original planting of cedars began to die from pollution generated by nearby factories in the early part of the twentieth century and were replaced by laurel oaks *(Quercus laurifolia)*. In 1990, cedar trees were once again planted along Cedar Avenue by the Moravian Church as part of the restoration of the historic landscape.

The townspeople's concern for the graveyard's appearance was also frequently mentioned in Moravian Church records.

A large ginkgo tree (Ginkgo biloba) *growing in God's Acre.*

(Opposite page) A late nineteenth-century photograph of Cedar Avenue along the west side of God's Acre. The fence between the avenue and the graveyard (right) was erected in 1887 to prevent residents from riding their horses through the graveyard. A stone wall replaced the picket fence on the west side of the avenue (left) in 1902.

April 18, 1787: In order to get good grass on the graveyard, we thought that it would be necessary to fertilize & spade those places where there are no graves so far and sow good grass seed on them this fall.

October 22, 1805: It is time to spread the quarters in the graveyard with manure. The weeds in the paths shall be loosened with a hoe so that they freeze this winter. Next spring tanning bark shall be covering the paths. The hedges will need repair too.

March 26, 1811: To beautify God's Acre on the east Bro. Christ shall plant cedar trees at the corners of the squares.

❧ The Landscape Today

Evidence of Salem's rich garden history flourishes today throughout the restored landscape. It can be seen among the many native trees and shrubs growing along the streets and walkways and inhabiting the lush green expanses which separate the quiet historic district from its modern urban surroundings. History lives in the small orchards, in the antique varieties of fruit trees, such as Maiden Blush and Buckingham apples, once staples on many southern homesteads, but now, sadly, no longer to be found among their more glossy modern cousins that currently line the produce counters at most retail outlets. Neat, colorful kitchen gardens, brimming with heirloom varieties of vegetables with such descriptive names as oxheart carrots or wren's egg beans, and old-time cottage flowers such as hollyhocks, larkspur, and cockscomb vividly reflect gardens of a bygone era.

Today, a staff of gardeners researches, plants, and maintains the gardens and landscape, relying on historical methods of cultivation whenever possible, but also prudently employing contemporary techniques, not readily apparent to the visitor, when required. Trucks, modern lawn care equipment, and a behind-the-scenes greenhouse play a role where necessary, but historical cultural practices are easily recognized within the gardens. These include the intensive use of garden space and the particular manner in which the gardens are arranged as indicated in the early landscape views of the town, the use of wide planting beds, and the reliance on old varieties of plants believed to have been in cultivation prior to 1850. An emphasis on good horticultural practice, including the careful monitoring and management of soil fertility, also continues to be of

Angel's trumpet (Dactura inoxia).

(Opposite page) Sweet autumn clematis (Clematis ternifolia) *blooming along a fence in the Volz field. This non-native clematis has naturalized throughout Salem.*

(Above) *Globe amaranth and cockscomb grow in a border bed of the Leinbach garden, while summer vegetables occupy one of the main planting squares. A castor bean plant* (Ricinus communis) *rises above the fence in the adjacent garden.*

(Above left) *A costumed interpreter harvests peas in the Triebel garden.*

(Bottom left) *Blackhaw blooming behind the Fourth House.*

primary concern and can be appreciated by the abundant harvests of the small family gardens.

Because of its multiple functions as an educational museum and thriving historical neighborhood, Old Salem's historical landscape is maintained in a manner that is more consistent or fastidious than would have been common in the late eighteenth or early nineteenth century. For example, a quick examination of late nineteenth-century photographs of the town reveals that mud was among the most notable primary landscape features of the time; however, it would not be understood or appreciated today given the existing context of the historic district. Fur-

In a late-nineteenth-century photograph of Church Street, mud stands out as a primary feature in the historical landscape. Outbuildings, fencing, and laundry are also significant landscape elements.

thermore, in the effort to show as much variety as possible in the re-created family gardens and provide a local example of horticultural excellence that might inspire visitors, it is entirely possible that the garden season and harvest are extended more than would have been normal for the period interpreted. In this one can only surmise what may have been common in Salem, although written reports of the town from travelers often give glowing accounts of the abundance of gardens and flowers and imply that despite its backcountry location, it was a place of considerable horticultural sophistication.

The Cape Fear Bank garden lies dormant under the snow.

❧ A Garden Calendar

A snake-rail fence delineates the boundary of Salem's historic district.

Winter

The garden season actually begins in the depth of winter as the horticulture staff develops garden plans for the coming season and orders any additional seed that may be necessary. Because each re-created family garden reflects the date of interpretation for its accompanying house, plant varieties and cultivars are selected according to their date of introduction; only those types of plants that were grown at the time represented by the particular garden are used. This necessitates the growing of what are commonly referred to as "heirloom variety" or "antique" plants, which frequently differ significantly from those readily available in the nursery trade and commonly grown in gardens today.

While garden plans are being finalized, some of the season's earliest plants which will be planted in the spring are sown in the greenhouse or cold frame. Last year's cuttings or divisions are moved into larger pots for transplanting into the gardens later in the season.

The pruning of fruit trees, such as apple, peach, cherry, and pear, takes place in Salem during late February or early March; most of the prunings are saved for later use in the garden as staking material or for trellising peas. Later in March grapevines, including the native muscadine and Catawba, receive their annual pruning, along with the currants and gooseberries that grow in some of the gardens. While their buds are still tight on the stems and the plants remain dormant, grafting wood, referred to as scion wood, is selected from some of the many antique varieties of apples already growing in the historic district. These will be grafted onto purchased rootstock later in the month. In this way Old Salem maintains a diverse collection of historical apple varieties for planting and replacement.

Spring

As late winter gives way to early spring, work in the gardens proceeds as weather and soil conditions allow. Perennial plants in the gardens are groomed, divided, and moved if required. Protective layers of winter mulch are raked back from empty beds, allowing the soil to warm in anticipation of early seeding, which will follow in the coming weeks. Fallow beds may be worked if the soil is not too wet, and any beds that require organic matter in the form of compost may receive it at this time.

The Cape Fear Bank garden in summer.

The success of Salem's re-created gardens is largely due to a sustained effort of soil building and fertility management, made possible largely by generous and regular applications of compost. The horticulture staff recycles all organic matter not contaminated by noxious perennial weeds through a process of composting. Plant material from the gardens, annual garden weeds, and leaves from throughout the district are collected together in piles and allowed to decompose for a period of about one year. Since all of the museum's exhibition gardens are re-creations, the soil condition of the beds at the time of construction varied, but largely consisted of common red clay fill that has since been transformed to rich loam as a direct result of the compost. Numerous Moravian references mention the amending of garden soil with animal manure, but since large quantities of animal manure are no longer readily available within the community, a plant-based compost serves as our modern-day equivalent.

Many vegetables are seeded directly into the garden beds in the early spring while nighttime frosts are still common. Peas, lettuce, spinach, beets, and turnips are a few of the first crops to go into the gardens. Irish or white potatoes are also planted early in the season, along with onions and young transplants of cabbage, cauliflower, and broccoli.

Flax is the first field crop to be planted in the early spring. Broadcast onto soil that was prepared the previous fall and only lightly cultivated just prior to planting to discourage any weeds that might get a head start on the crop, the seed is pressed into the fresh seedbed by rolling. It generally sprouts soon thereafter, while other crops are still waiting for warmer weather. Flax is one of the many traditional field crops grown in Salem today as it was two hundred years ago.

GARDEN SEEDS,

Long expected, but come at last!

THE subscriber has just received from Baltimore, an additional supply of fresh Garden Seeds, among which are the following:

BEANS,	Drumhead
Large rob roy	Large green glazed.
Red marrow	Red and white Celery
dun colored or Quaker	Early Silecia Lettuce
Dwarf white cranberry	Grand Admiral do
White Dutch pole	Early Malta do
Cranberry snaps	Tennisbal do
Horticultural.	Sugar loaf do
Sinclair Beet	Lazy do
CABBAGE	Large white head do
Dwarf Paris	Paris white Onion
Cribbs' early york	Bishop's early dw'f Peas
Early sugar loaf	Rhubarb, for pies
Flat Dutch	Salsify or vegetable oyster
	JOHN C. BLUM.

Salem, April 28.　　　　18

Advertisement for garden seeds that ran in the May 14, 1836, issue of the Weekly Chronicle and Farmers' Register, *one of the newspapers in Salem published by John Christian Blum (1784–1854). Blum also began to publish* Blum's Almanac *in 1828 and, as this ad indicates, engaged in the sideline of selling seeds. Some of the varieties listed are grown in the gardens today, including 'Flat Dutch' cabbage, 'Drumhead' cabbage, 'Tennisball' lettuce, and salsify.*

From top to bottom: 'Tom Thumb,' 'Schweitzer's Mescher Bibb,' and 'Tennisball' lettuces.

The last frost of the season occurs, on average, around the middle of April. After that time, the pace of work in the garden quickens, with digging, planting, thinning, amending the soil, weeding, and cultivating taking place simultaneously. The garden season is well underway, with lots of work to be done.

By this time the peas that were planted a month earlier stretch skyward with their grasping tendrils, searching for something on which to climb. If not already in place, the fruit tree prunings from the previous month are stuck into the bed between the rows of peas to offer support for the rapidly growing plants. This practice of growing peas on sticks cannot be directly attributed to the Moravians in Salem but, based on recommendations in early gardening books of the period, it probably was a common practice.

While the supports for the peas are being put into place, supports for climbing or pole beans can be erected in preparation for their planting in the weeks to come. An early photograph of a garden in Salem, believed to have been taken in the late nineteenth century, contains an example of a similar type of trellising (see page 90). Though the photograph is of a later period than the re-created museum gardens, it shows a local example of a specific garden technique that probably predates the photograph. In the absence of any other evidence, Salem gardeners continue to employ this method of growing beans.

By the beginning of May all chance of a late frost is past, and the season for planting warm-season crops arrives. Young plants of peppers, winter and summer squash, and cucumbers are removed from cold frames and set out into gardens. Beans, both pole and bush varieties, are planted in gardens at this time as well. Yellow pear and red pear tomato varieties are planted in the later-period gardens, since these are not believed to have been grown in Salem until the mid-nineteenth century.

Much of the produce grown within the gardens is used by Old Salem's domestic skills department for cooking demonstrations. Fresh fruits and vegetables are prepared daily in the kitchens of many exhibit buildings, using traditional recipes and techniques. Garden surplus is frequently dried, pickled, or stored in root cellars for use during the winter months.

The spring season reaches a virtual crescendo of color and fragrance during late May and early June. Naturalized throughout Old Salem, blue and purple bachelor's buttons, larkspur, and garden phlox bloom abundantly in the gardens as well as in undisturbed areas throughout the historic district. In the gardens spring-bloomers such as sweet William, pinks, tree peonies, and Florentine iris conclude their annual display, while flowers of zinnias, hollyhocks, coreopsis, and globe amaranth begin to come forth. Many of the antique-variety roses grown in Old Salem bloom during this period, including the apothecary rose, the dog rose, and the fragrant damask rose. Shrubs and small trees like Carolina allspice, blackhaw, and fringetree bloom in the yards and wooded fields.

Peaches 'Late Crawford.'

Summer

As summer approaches, preparation for planting field crops commences. In keeping with historical precedent, maize, pumpkins, broom corn, cotton, and tobacco continue to be grown in Salem in order to interpret the agricultural traditions that were historically carried out by the Moravians on their leased outlots or on nearby farms. Another benefit of growing these crops today is that it gives Old Salem's interpretive staff the opportunity to demonstrate some of the techniques associated with the growing of these crops, as well as providing raw materials for cooking demonstrations, broom making, threshing, rye-basket making, spinning, and tobacco processing.

A member of Old Salem's domestic skills staff harvests flax by carefully pulling the plants from the soil with the roots still intact. Further processing of the plant fibers produces the material from which linen fabric is made.

These agricultural crops are now grown, among other places, in the Volz House field on Main Street a few blocks south of the square. Laid off as a small farm in 1816 for the retired farmer Johannes Volz, this field serves today as an agricultural demonstration area for growing traditional crops.

The last of the major spring garden crops reach maturity and are harvested by mid-June, but successive sowings of summer crops, including beans, squash, and cucumbers, continue throughout the month. Several varieties of gourds, including calabash, dipper, and bottle gourds, are planted along fences. By summer's end they will have covered the structures and hang heavy with the hard-shelled fruits that will be dried for storage containers and other useful objects over the winter. Intensive cultivating to control weeds, mulching to conserve soil moisture, and deadheading to prolong blooming time occur throughout the summer while fruits and vegetables are harvested as they ripen.

Costumed interpreters with sickles and scythes harvest winter crops of rye and wheat that ripen in the fields during the early part of the summer, and stack the sheaths into the characteristic shocks which were once a common sight, dotting the rural agricultural landscape, at this time of year. The flax that was planted late in the winter or early spring is ready for harvest in early summer and is carefully pulled from the soil, roots still intact, and arranged in small bundles in the grass where it will begin its retting process (literally a process of partial decomposition) whereby the outer covering of the stalk and the pith are allowed to decompose, leaving only the stronger flax fibers for further processing into linen cloth later in the year.

As summer draws to a close, apples litter the ground in many of the gardens, and the preparation for the fall growing season begins. Seedlings of cabbage, broccoli, cauliflower, and celery, started under shade in a nursery bed, await transplanting into the garden sometime between mid-August and mid-September. During this same period of time, fall crops of lettuce, beets, turnips, spinach, kohlrabi, mustard, and kale may be planted. Since Old Salem's growing season generally lasts well into November, fall gardens are frequently some of the most productive of the year. Their challenge, however, lies in the irony that the cool-loving plants must be started and become established during what is frequently the hottest part of the year, the last days of August.

Fall

Spring-flowering perennials may be cut back and divided throughout the fall, and many summer flowers continue to bloom, some showing renewed vigor with the cooler temperatures. Zinnias, portulaca, coreopsis, verbena, and tall red cockscomb hold their blossoms well into the fall, when New England asters and goldenrod make their annual debut. Spring bulbs, including numerous species of narcissus, old varieties of tulips, and Roman hyacinths are planted this time of year, having been dug and divided in the summer as soon as their foliage died back. Seeds of many flowering plants, both vegetables and ornamentals, ripen during the fall and are gathered at that time for processing and storage later in the winter.

Pumpkin, 'Rouge vif d'Étampes.'

Old Salem gardeners gather and save most of their own seed from one year to the next, since many of the old varieties are difficult to locate—if available at all—through conventional seed sources. These open-pollinated varieties, unlike modern hybrid types, produce seeds that are true to type year after year, making it possible to collect, grow, and preserve these living garden legacies for perpetuity.

Cooler fall temperatures allow for the planting of winter grains such as winter wheat, oats, rye and spelt, an ancient grain similar to the wheat that was grown by the Moravians during the early years of settlement. Cotton, tobacco, and broom corn are harvested as they reach maturity and stored in the barn for processing later in the season. Fall is also the preferred season for setting out trees, especially the fruit trees that were grafted the previous spring and have since put on several feet of growth while residing in a nursery bed over the summer.

Fall vegetables continue to produce well in the gardens through Thanksgiving and during warmer years up until Christmas. As crops are harvested, compost is often applied to the soil if it is required. Other areas of the garden may receive a protective layer of leaf mulch for the winter.

In December and January, work in the gardens themselves slows considerably, but some cleaning up of the residue from the previous season's crops may be undertaken as the weather allows. Seeds are dried, cleaned, and packaged for next year's use and tools may be repaired, cleaned, and put away for the season. The staff reviews the successes and failures of the previous growing season and considers preliminary plans for the gardens of the coming year.

Spider flower (Cleome hasslerana), *cockscomb, and four-o'clocks* (Mirabilis jalapa) *grow alongside carrots and squash in the Leinbach garden in late summer. Joe-Pye weed* (Eupatorium maculatum) *blooms in the rear.*

❧ Conclusion

Salem's restored historical landscape is the product of considerable research and careful management. Though visually attractive throughout the year with a variety of plant material and interesting landscape elements, it offers much more than a historical context in which to view the restored architecture. For the reflective visitor it contributes to an understanding of the aesthetic sensibility of a community of individuals for whom careful land-use planning, self-reliance, and a firm commitment to place contributed to the creation of a landscape within the wilderness which was unequaled in this part of the country. It remains a landscape in which the simple ideals of order and utility combine to create an outdoor environment of natural beauty uniquely reminiscent of the Moravian founders for whom the virtues of hard work, piety, service to others, and pride of craftsmanship were practiced as a daily devotion to God.

Coreopsis (Corcopsis lanceolata) *and rose campion* (Lychnis coronaria).

Cabbage, 'Savoy Drumhead.'

❧ Appendix: *The Bethabara Plant Lists*

The plans of the Upland Garden (1759) and the Hortus Medicus (1761), pictured on pages 23 and 25, together with the legends indicating names and locations of the plants that were cultivated there at that time, offer a very early picture of gardening practices in colonial America. The plans and plant lists are the work of Christian Gottlieb Reuter, whose old German script is evident. The plant names are often given in both Latin and German, and sometimes in German alone.

Translations of the plant lists that appear below were made between 1975 and 1979 by the late Dr. h.c. Gerd Krüssmann, at that time director of the Botanical Garden in Dortmund, Germany. Dr. Krüssmann is considered by many to be the world's leading horticultural expert in the second half of the twentieth century.

The translations give both the common and botanical names. Modern botanical names listed are those given in *Hortus Third* (1976), by the L. H. Bailey Hortorium. Current names appear in parentheses; older names (synonyms) are in brackets. In 1979, Dr. Frederick G. Meyer, then supervisory botanist in charge of the herbarium of the National Arboretum in Washington, D.C., reviewed the modern botanical names for accuracy. In 1995 Dr. Arthur O. Tucker, research botanist at Delaware State University, checked and updated the botanical names.

The Upland Garden

As it was laid out by Bro. Lung and has now been planted. Bethabara. Contains ½ Acres, 26 rods. The 1st of May 1759.

Explanation of the Large Letters

The large letters are on the borders and the walks, where you find:

A. Horseradish *(Armoracia rusticana) [Cochlearia armoracia]*

B. Asparagus *(Asparagus officinalis)* and onions *(Allium cepa)*

C. Parsley, curly *(Petroselinum crispum)*

D. Garlic *(Allium sativum)* and thyme *(Thymus vulgaris)*

E. Last year's parsley

F. Cloves (probably a *Dianthus plumarius* hybrid)

G. Black beans *(Phaseolus vulgaris)*

H. Still more parsley

I. At the summer house, flowers: daffodils *(Narcissus pseudonarcissus)*, cloves, and lilacs *(Syringa vulgaris)*

K. Gooseberries *(Ribes uva-crispa), [R. grossularia]* and hops *(Humulus lupulus)*

L. Gateway with grapes.

M. Little garden house

N. Two grass (or sod) banks

O. Live hedge of dogwood (blood-twig or European, *Cornus sanguinea),* only one year old.

Explanation of the Colors

1. The green sections and the beds are the vegetable plots.

2. The seed plots and the border beds are reddish.

3. All walks and paths have been left white.

4. The rest is to be seen from the preceding and the following:

Explanation of the Numbers and Small Letters

1, 2, 3a. Lettuce *(Lactuca sativa)*

   b. Sweet peas *(Pisum sativum var. sativum)*

4, 5. Carrots *(Daucus carota var. sativus)* and parsnips *(Pastinaca sativa)*

6. Parsnips

7. Planted mangolds *(Beta vulgaris)*

9. Melons and Spanish pepper *(Cucumis melo, Reticulatus* group) Chili pepper, red pepper *(Capsicum annuum, Longum* group)

10a. Grafted quince stems (*Cydonia oblonga*)

    b. An early bed

    c. A quince tree nursery

    d. A cabbage bed (*Brassica oleracea, Capitata* group)

8. This section is planted only with seed that was brought personally from Germany, namely:

    a. Parsley

    b. Turnip-rooted parsley, Hamburg parsley (*P. crispum*, var. *tuberosum*)

    c. Onions

    d. Red cabbage

    e. Beets (*Beta vulgaris*)

    f. Celery (*Apium graveolens*, var. *dulce*)

    h. "Kerbel," possibly chervil (*Anthriscus cerefolium*)

    g. Field salad or corn salad (*Valerianella locusta*) [*V. olitoria*]

    i. Spinach (*Spinacia olercea*)

    k. Garlic

    l. Mangolds

    m. Cress (*Lepidium sativum*)

    n. Red cabbage

    o. Radish (*Raphanus sativus*)

    p. Cauliflower (*Brassica oleracea, Botrytis* group)

    q. [Illegible]

    r. Cabbage

    s. Spoonwort, scurvy grass (*Cochlearia officinalis*)

    t. Capper-seeds of nasturtium, "Kaper" (*Tropaeolum majus, T. minus*)

    u. Kohlrabi (*Brassica oleracea, Gongyloces* group)

    v. Marjoram (*Origanum majorana*), [*Majorana hortensis*]

    w.

    x. Empty, to be used for transplanting

Hortus Medicus

At Bethabara, in the year 1761. As this one is planted this year by Brother August Schubert. June 23.

1. and 2. Curly mint (*Mentha spicata* 'Crispa' or *Mentha aquatica* 'Crispa')

3. Seed of anise (*Pimpinella anisum*)

4. Spanish cress, nasturtium (*Tropaeolum majus, T. minus*)

5. Seed of fennel (*Foeniculum vulgare*)

6. Spanish cress, nasturtium

7, 8. Seed of caraway (*Carum carvi*)

9. a. Mugwort (*Artemisia vulgaris*)

    b. Violet (*Viola odorata*)

    c. Seed of caraway

10. Lavender (*Lavandula angustifolia*) [*L. officinalis, L. vera, L. spica*]

11. Seed of dill (*Anethum graveolens*)

12. Common centaury (*Centaurium erythraea*) [*C. minus, C. umbellatum*]

13. Sage (*Salvia officinalis*)

14. Same

15, 16. Mugwort

17, 18, 19. Sorrel (*Rumex acetosa*)

20. Yarrow (*Achillea millefolium*)

21. Empty

22. Dog rose (*Rosa canina*)

23. Curly parsley (*Petroselinum crispum*)

24. Larkspur (*Consolida regalis*) [*Delphinum consolida*]

25. Empty

26, 27, 28. Southernwood (*Artemisia abrotanum*)

29, 30. Sweet basil (*Ocinum basilicum*), and sweet marjoram (*Origanum majorana*) [*Majorana hortensis*]

31, 32, 33. Southernwood

34. Empty

35. Larkspur

36. Empty

37. White poppy or opium poppy (*Papaver somniferum*)

38, 39. Empty

40. Columbine (*Aquilegia vulgaris*) and red, field, or corn poppy (*Papaver rhoeas*)

41, 42. Seed of red poppy

43. Angelica (*Angelica archangelica*) [*A. officinalis*]

44. Yarrow

45. Safflower, wild saffron (*Carthamus tinctorious*)

46. a. St. Mary's thistle (*Silybum marianum*), [*Carduus marianus*]

    b. Fumitory (*Fumaria officinalis*)

47. and 48. Lovage (*Levisticum officinale*)

49. Angelica

50. Sorrel

51. Fumitory

52. Red chamomile (species unknown), white or madonna lily

(Lilium album), and rhubarb *(Rheum rhabarbarum), [R. rhaponticum]*

53. White lilies

54. Roses: red and white (apothecary rose, *Rosa gallica* 'Officinalis'); *(Rosa alba,* white rose)

55. a. Seed of citrus (maybe true citron, *Citrus medica)*
    b. Spanish vetch (Possibly sweet peas, *Lathyrus odoratus)*

56. Red roses

57. White lilies

58. Roman chamomile *(Chamaemelum nobile) [Anthemis nobilis]*, and seed of coriander *(Coriandrum sativum)*

59. Plantain *(Plantago minor)* and lungwort *(Pulmonaria officinalis)*

60. Wormseed, old-woman *(Artemisia maritima)*

61. Lavender and hormium *(Salvia viridis)*

62. Fennel flower *(Nigella sativa)* and "Perfoliata," probably alexanders *(Smyrnium perfoliatum)*

63. Scurvy grass *(Cochlearia officinalis)* and lavender

64. White poppies

65. Hyssop *(Hyssopus officinalis)*

66. Larkspur

67. Daisy, probably English daisy *(Bellis perennis)*

68. Hyssop amd Roman chamomile

69. Sage and daisy

70. "Perfoliata"

71. Blessed thistle *(Cnicus benedictus) [Carduus benedictus]*

72. Scurvy grass

73. Salsify *(Tragopogon porrifolium)*

74. Balm *(Melissa officinalis)*

75. Wormwood *(Artemisia absinthium)*

76. Rue *(Ruta graveolens)*

77. Tansy *(Tanacetum vulgare), [Chrysanthemum vulgare]*

78. Poppies that wandered

79. Wild chamomile *(Matricaria recutita) [M. chamomilla]*

80. Scabiosa *(Scabiosa atropurpurea)* and betony *(Stachys officinalis), [Betonica officinalis]*

81. Borage *(Borago officinalis)* and sage

82. Sage

83. Wild chamomile

84. Wild chamomile and daisy

85, 86, 87. Marshmallow *(Althaea officinalis)*

88. Comfrey *(Symphytum officinale)*

89. Marshmallow

90. Elecampane *(Inula helenium)* and sweet clover, melilot *(Melilotus officinalis)*

91. Scorzonera *(Scorzonera hispanica)*

92. Poppy, wild

93. Seed of columbine

94. Melons, muskmelons *(Cucumis melo, Reticulatus* group)

95. Cucumbers *(Cucumis sativas)*

96. Comfrey

A. The little garden house built in 1759 by Triebel
B. Terraces

TOM FINDING OUT ABOUT OLD SALEM MAY 1894

Photographer Tom Hege (second from left) interviewing Salem residents in 1894. The garden behind them is located along Academy Street just east of the Single Brothers' slaughterhouse, now demolished. Note the pole structure in the garden, probably for trellising beans.

❧ Bibliography

All quotations, unless otherwise identified, are from documents in the Archives of the Moravian Church in America, Southern Province, Winston-Salem, North Carolina. Most of these are found in the *Records of the Moravians in North Carolina* listed below; documents translated from German appear in the form used in those volumes. For documents in German that are not reproduced in the *Records,* the author has relied on unpublished translations produced for Old Salem by Erika Huber and Edmund Schwarze, now on file in the Archives of the Moravian Church in America, Southern Province, Winston-Salem, North Carolina.

Quotations in the text labeled "Bethlehem Archives" are from unpublished letters translated by Edmund Schwarze for Old Salem now on file in the Archives of the Moravian Church of America, Northern Province, Bethlehem, Pennsylvania.

Bynum, Flora Ann L. *Old Salem Garden Guide.* Winston-Salem, N. C.: Old Salem, Inc., 1979.

———. "Father of American Mycology." *Three Forks of Muddy Creek* II (1975): 41–50.

———. "Old-World Gardens in the New World: The Gardens of the Moravian Settlement of Bethabara in North Carolina, 1753–1772." *Journal of Garden History* XVI, no. 2 (1996).

Capps, Gene. "Meat For the Tables of Wachovia." *Three Forks of Muddy Creek* II (1975): 3–6.

Conner, Juliana Margaret. Diary, 1827. Typescript. Ms. 174, Southern Historical Collection. University of North Carolina Library, Chapel Hill.

Hatch, Peter. "The Forester in Early Salem." *Three Forks of Muddy Creek* IV (1977): 14–18.

Hinman, William. "Phillip Christian Gottleib Reuter, First Surveyor of Wachovia." M.A. thesis, Wake Forest University, 1985.

Hodgson, Anne. "A Short History of Salem Square." *Three Forks of Muddy Creek* XIV (1990): 24–37.

Hymnal and Liturgies of the Moravian Church. Bethlehem, Pa.: Provincial Synod of the Moravian Church, 1920.

Kramsch, Samuel. "Flora of Salem," 1789 (two versions); "Flora of Salem," 1789–1791. Trans. Erika Huber, 1950–1952; with botanical identifications by Dr. R. L. Wyatt, 1975. Archives of the Moravian Church in America, Southern Province, Winston-Salem, N.C.

Kremer, Eliza Vierling. Reminiscences, n.d. Moravian Archives, Winston-Salem.

Leinbach, John Henry. Diaries, 1830–1843. Moravian Archives, Winston-Salem.

Liberty Hyde Bailey Hortorium, *Hortus Third.* New York: Macmillan, 1976.

Lineback, Julius A. "The Single Brethren's House in Salem, North Carolina." In *Salem's Remembrancers,* ed. Edwin L. Stockton, Jr. Winston-Salem, N.C.: Wachovia Historical Society, 1976, 80–106.

Martin, William D. *The Journal of William D. Martin: A Journey from South Carolina to Connecticut in the Year 1809.* Charlotte, N.C.: Heritage House, 1959.

Old Salem Official Guidebook. Winston-Salem, N.C.: Old Salem, Inc., 1982.

Records of the Moravians in North Carolina. Vols. I–VII, ed. Adelaide L. Fries; vol. VIII, ed. Douglas L. Rights: vol. IX, ed. Minnie J. Smith; vols. X–XI, ed. Kenneth G. Hamilton. Raleigh: North Carolina Departmentof Archives and History, 1922–1969.

Reuter, Phillip Christian Gottlieb. Memoir, c. 1759–61. Moravian Archives, Winston-Salem.

———. Survey notes, 1764. Moravian Archives, Winston-Salem.

———. Wachovia Land Register. Notes, 1760. Moravian Archives, Winston-Salem.

Schweinitz, Lewis David. "Flora Salemitana." Library, Academy of Natural Sciences of Philadelphia.

———. Papers. Library, Academy of Natural Sciences of Philadelphia.

———. *Synopsis Fungorium in America Boreali media de Gentium* (A Summary of Fungi Growing in Northern Mid-America). Philadelphia: American Philosophical Society, 1834.

Smith, Andrew F. *The Tomato in America: Early History, Culture, and Cookery.* Columbia: University of South Carolina Press, 1994.

Smith, William Loughton. *The Journal of William Loughton Smith, 1790–1791.* Boston: Massachusetts Historical Society, 1917.

❧ *Photography Credits and Acknowledgments*

Photographs by Virginia Weiler: pages vi, viii, 3, 5, 6, 7, 8 (bottom), 9, 10, 11, 13, 14, 17, 18, 19, 21, 24, 28, 29, 33, 35, 36, 39 (top and bottom), 40, 41, 43 (top), 45, 46, 47, 48, 49, 55 (top and bottom), 57, 60, 64, 65, 66 (top and bottom), 68, 69, 70, 72, 73, 74 (all), 76, 77, 78, 80, 81, 82, 83, 84, 85, 86, 93.

The following are reproduced with the permission of the organizations and individuals listed below. Unless otherwise noted, all photographs are Old Salem file photographs.

Old Salem, Inc.: Historic photographs on pages 8 (top), 34, 38, 42, 71, 75, 90; Reuter surveying instruments, page 27; maps, drawings and prints on pages 4, 32, 44, 52, 53; Blum advertisement, page 79. Pages 4, 27, and 32, photographed by Wesley Stewart.

The Wachovia Historical Society, Winston-Salem, North Carolina: von Redeken, *View of Salem,* title page; and Welfare, *Salem from the Southwest* on page 2. Photographed by Wesley Stewart.

Moravian Archives, Herrnhut, Germany: Reuter's map of Wachovia, page 16; and "Prospect of Bethabara," page 22.

Archives of the Moravian Church in America, Northern Province, Bethlehem, Pennsylvania: Reuter, Upland Garden plan, page 23.

Archives of the Moravian Church in America, Southern Province, Winston-Salem, North Carolina: Reuter maps and plans on pages 20, 25, 26, 31, 43 (bottom), 61. Photographed by Wesley Stewart.

Archives, Salem Academy and College: Christina Kramsch watercolors, pages 50, 59 (photographed by Wesley Stewart); historic photograph, page 51.

Library, the Academy of Natural Sciences of Philadelphia: von Schweinitz watercolors, pages 56, 58.

A special thanks to two private collectors who have graciously allowed their works to be included: *A View of Salem from the Northwest,* artist unknown, page 12; and Elias Vogler, *A View of Salem Square,* page 62.

Fig tree (Ficus carica 'Magnolia').

The Gardens of Salem was designed and typeset by Kachergis Book Design in Pittsboro, North Carolina. The typeface, Adobe Minion, was designed by Robert Slimbach and reflects the classical typography of the late Renaissance.

The color separations for *The Gardens of Salem* were prepared by R. R. Donnelley and Sons Company in Willard, Ohio, and by WSS Graphic Imaging in Raleigh, North Carolina. The book was printed on 80-pound Patina Matte and bound by R. R. Donnelley and Sons Company in Reynosa, Mexico.